REI...

Dear Mom and Dad,

But by the afternoon? You were gone. And Dad, you'd get meaner as the night went on, spitting words like venom, yelling at me for things I didn't even understand. You both put so much on me that no kid should ever have to carry. And the worst part? I thought it was normal. I thought every family was like this. I thought every house had a liquor cabinet that never ran dry. I thought everybody's parents drank all the time. I thought every family lived in separate corners of the same home, avoiding each other, except when the alcohol took over and made you loud, affectionate, or cruel. I thought this was just how families worked.

JEREMY ALLEN DAMOURS

READING *DEAR RED STRAW* BY JEREMY DAMOURS

AN HONEST TESTAMENT TO SURVIVAL, TRAUMA, AND RECLAMATION

Jeremy Damours' *Dear Red Straw* is not just a memoir—it is a luminous, gut-wrenching portrait of life forged in the shadows of addiction. Written with lyrical precision and fearless vulnerability, this powerful work explores how trauma shapes identity, how silence masks survival, and how storytelling can liberate even the most hidden parts of ourselves. It is a deeply personal yet universally resonant account of growing up in a home consumed by alcoholism, and the long journey toward clarity, healing, and wholeness.

From the very first page, readers are invited into a household ruled by the rhythms of drinking and denial. The eponymous "red straw" becomes a haunting symbol—one that encapsulates the desperate pursuit of control in a world unraveling. This small object, innocuous in appearance, commands immense emotional power. Its presence determines peace or chaos in Damours' childhood home, setting the stage for a memoir that uses objects, memories, and everyday moments to anchor the emotional complexity of growing up in dysfunction.

What makes *Dear Red Straw* stand apart from other memoirs in the addiction genre is its unflinching honesty. Damours does not sensationalize his story, nor does he sanitize it. Instead, he writes with precision and tenderness about the gray areas of love, trauma, and memory. His parents are portrayed not as villains, but as deeply flawed people battling demons of their own. His father's alcoholism, often filtered through quiet routines and terrifying outbursts, is mirrored by a mother who drifts between presence and absence—offering help one moment, lost in her own haze the next.

The book is structured in chapters that feel like emotional snapshots—scenes that capture not just what happened, but how it felt. There's the pain of a child performing for drunken parents who barely notice, the heartbreak of watching a father refuse treatment after a dementia diagnosis, and the paralyzing shame of trying to appear "normal" in a small town that sees everything and says nothing. Through it all, Damours' voice remains steady, even as it recounts moments that would break many.

A particularly moving aspect of the memoir is the inclusion of Damours' inner life as he comes to terms with his identity and sense of worth. The reader is given access to his thoughts as a boy grappling with queerness, as a teenager fearing rejection, and as a man trying to navigate love while unlearning the emotional strategies that once kept him safe. These threads are woven into the broader narrative without ever overshadowing the central storyline. Instead, they add rich layers that make the memoir feel complete, multifaceted, and real.

At its heart, *Dear Red Straw* is not a story of blame, but of reckoning. It's about what it means to grow up when your parents are the ones you have to recover from. It's about realizing that trauma doesn't end when you leave the house—it evolves, often hiding itself in adult relationships, careers, and patterns of self-worth. Yet Damours handles these revelations with grace, never indulging in pity but instead focusing on insight and growth.

The prose is both poetic and accessible. Damours writes with a restraint that underscores the power of what's left unsaid. His reflections are sharp and often beautifully phrased, carrying weight without melodrama. There are moments of lightness, too—humor, affection, and a deep appreciation for small mercies. And though the story is filled with pain, it is never hopeless. Damours offers the reader glimpses of redemption: in love, in therapy, in chosen family, and most of all, in telling the truth.

One of the most poignant sections of the book is his farewell to his father—a scene filled with contradictions: anger and empathy, sorrow and relief. The description of that final hospital visit, of holding back tears and bracing against finality, is among the most emotionally powerful moments in the memoir. And it is in this moment, perhaps more than any other, that the reader sees Damours for who he is—a survivor, yes, but also a seeker. Someone willing to dig through the wreckage of memory not just to find peace, but to reclaim meaning.

The red straw, seen at first as a symbol of fear and control, takes on deeper meaning by the end of the book. It becomes a stand-in for all the ways people try to keep themselves together when everything else is falling apart. It is a symbol of addiction, yes—but also of ritual, dependency, and the illusion of stability. By examining it so closely, Damours doesn't just tell us about his past—he invites us to reflect on the objects, habits, and silences in our own lives that carry more weight than we often admit.

In *Dear Red Straw*, Jeremy Damours has written something remarkable. This book does what all the best memoirs do: it takes personal pain and shapes it into something readers can hold, learn from, and feel deeply. It's a story that will resonate with anyone who has ever felt unseen, anyone who has had to rebuild their sense of self from scratch, and anyone searching for beauty in the midst of brokenness.

It's not an easy read—but it's an essential one. Honest, intelligent, and beautifully told, *Dear Red Straw* is a gift to those learning how to tell their own stories—and a quiet beacon for those still learning how to listen.

Lynette Grenfield,
CEO, Limelight Publishing, 2025

DEAR RED STRAW

JEREMY ALLEN DAMOURS

LIMELIGHT PUBLISHING
LULU PRESS

Dear Red Straw

First published in the United States
by Lulu Press
And in Australia
by Limelight Publishing
© Jeremy Allen Damours

Limelight Publishing PTY LTD
Po Box 65, Narangba, Queensland
Australia, 4504
limelightpublishing.com
1 2 4 4 0 7 7 4 8 1 9

Lulu Press/Publishing
PO Box 12018, Durham, NC
United States, 27709
lulu.com

No part of this publication may be reproduced, stored in a retrieval system, or transmitted in any form or by any means — electronic, mechanical, photocopying, recording, or otherwise — without the prior written permission of the publisher, except in the case of brief quotations embodied in critical articles or reviews. This book is a work of nonfiction. Every effort has been made to ensure that the information presented is accurate and current at the time of publication. However, the author and publisher make no representations or warranties regarding the completeness, accuracy, or reliability of the content. The information is provided for general informational purposes only and is not intended as professional advice. Readers are encouraged to consult qualified professionals for advice specific to their individual circumstances. The author and publisher disclaim any liability for any loss or damage incurred directly or indirectly by the use of the information contained in this book. For permissions or inquiries, please contact: lulu.com

Cover image: Limelight Publishing
Typeset: Limelight Publishing
Printed and bound in Australia
and the United States

ISBN: 978-1-326-25129-1

lulu.com/spotlight/jeremy-allen-damours
facebook.com/profile.php?id=61571489221322
instagram.com/jeremyallenauthor/
www.linkedin.com/in/jeremy-damours-9a568878

Contents

Prologue

Open Letter To The World, By An Alcoholic

Chapter 1: **The Normal That Wasn't** 1

Chapter 2: **Trapped On Edge** 27

Chapter 3: **Sworn To Secrecy** 57

Chapter 4: **Bound By Shame and Guilt** 89

Chapter 5: **Avoiding The Storm** 125

Chapter 6: **Blurred Lines** 155

Chapter 7: **Chasing The Reins** 185

Chapter 8: **Tangled Ties** 211

Chapter 9: **The Weight of Relapse** 239

Chapter 10: **When Death Moves In** 267

Chapter 11: **Standing Strong** 315

Dear Red Straw

Jeremy Allen Damours

Dedication

To Josh and Chris—

We've each found our own way—
some of us sooner, some still getting there.
But somehow, we've always stayed loosely connected,
even through the silence, the distance, the weight.

This book isn't about what we never said.
It's about finally recognizing what's always been there—
and using that truth to make something good from it.

These chapters are a mirror—
not just showing the story for what it was,
but reflecting the parts of you still living inside it.
The hurt and the resilience.
The cracks and the light.
What still feels unfinished—
and what could be your next step forward.

More was taken from us than we understood at the time.
But what's still here is a quiet invitation—
to become the kind of brothers we never had the space to be.

Dad's gone now.
And Mom—imperfect, complicated, still ours—is still here.
The past doesn't need our silence anymore.
What we do next is what matters now.

Acknowledgments

To my mother, Kathryn Damours—

I don't know if this book would exist without your permission.
And even now, I'm not sure why you gave it.

I struggled with the decision to write this—
not because the story wasn't mine to tell,
but because it was ours.
Personal. Messy. Still unfolding.

It's about growing up with two parents who drank—
what that did to a child,
and what that child had to unravel as an adult.
To tell that story honestly, I had to include you.
And that brought a kind of conflict that never quite left.

But when I came to you and asked,
you said yes.

You became a quiet historian for pieces I couldn't fully recall—
helping me piece together what was real,
what still hurts,
what I buried long ago.
For that, I'm grateful.

And I'm also proud—
of the path you're on now,
of the way you've taken ownership of your own story,
of the moments you've chosen sobriety
when the old patterns could have easily returned.

Your blessing means more than I'll ever be able to say.
And your honesty lives in these pages,
even if no one knows exactly where.

This book holds all of it—
the ache, the shame, the survival,
the history, and the hope.

Thank you for letting me tell it.

More By the Author

- *Grow Through What You Go Through: Everyday Calm, Everyday Strong*

- *Growing Through Chaos* (LinkedIn newsletter series)
www.linkedin.com/in/jeremy-damours-9a568878

- *Upcoming Collection* (Title Forthcoming)
(Adapted essays from the Growing Through Chaos series)

Prologue

Long after the drinking began, the skinny red straw appeared—silent, and destined to be obeyed.
Plastic. Harmless-looking.

And yet, for years, it held more power in the house than anyone else.

He'd taken a box of them home from a vendor he worked with—restaurant-grade, narrow, the kind that didn't bend. Over time, the box dwindled. When only one was left, he saved it like it was sacred.

And for years, it was the only one he used.
He washed it gently with warm soapy water. Blew air through it. Laid it out on a clean towel to dry.

The ritual was the same every day.
Once work ended, the drinking began.
If the red straw wasn't immediately within reach, chaos followed.

"Where the hell is my goddamn red straw?!"

The question wasn't really a question.
It was a warning.

Because even though he could drink without it, he didn't want to. And if it wasn't there, he'd make sure everyone knew it.

He'd raise his voice. Slam his fists. Curse.
And then the whole house would scramble—stomachs turning, hearts racing—trying to find the one object that might keep the night from falling apart.

We always found it.
Somehow, we always did.

The straw became the difference between peace and explosion.

She understood this—maybe better than anyone.

Even while she had her own habits—her own ways of disappearing, numbing, checking out—she knew how tightly he clung to that straw.

Most nights, she was already drifting—slurring her words, losing time, fumbling through the same loop of forgetfulness.

But when he started yelling, something in her would snap into place—just enough sobriety to scramble, to search, to smooth things over.

She knew the way that straw dictated the night. The trip. The air in the room.

And whether she meant to or not, she often played along.

Not because she believed in the ritual, but because she knew what happened when it failed.

Her presence was unreliable.
But her reaction to his rage was not.

The straw wasn't just about the drink.
It was about control.
About the performance of normalcy.
About needing one small thing to be exactly right,
even when everything else was broken.

Even on vacations, the straw came with him—wrapped and packed like a prized possession.

Once, in a hotel room, it wasn't there. He hadn't asked anyone to pack it.
But when it wasn't found, someone had to pay for it.

He told her to go downstairs, find a bartender, and not come back until she had the right one.
Skinny. Red. Exact.

She returned with a regular straw.
It wasn't good enough.

He stormed out, muttering about betrayal, and drank alone at the hotel bar for hours.

Strangely, he didn't seem to need the straw in public.
At the bar, around strangers, he could drink straight
from the glass. Calm. Unbothered.

But at home? With her? With the kids?
The straw mattered again.
The ritual returned.

And that was the pattern: rage reserved for the private
spaces. Rituals and blame woven into daily life.
The family tiptoeing around an object so small it could
disappear in a drawer—but never from their minds.

It was never really about the straw.
But it was always about the straw.

Open Letter To The World, By An Alcoholic

Hi, my name is Kathy, and I'm an alcoholic.

It still feels so strange to say the words "I'm an alcoholic." Strange because saying it out loud makes it real, like I can't hide from it anymore. It means finally admitting to myself and to others, family members, friends, etc., something so huge. Something that has been a part of my life for over four decades.

And being an alcoholic doesn't just mean I drink too much. It means I'm an addict. Alcohol became something my body and mind depended on. I wasn't just drinking because I wanted to, I was drinking because I had to. Because without it, my body would shake, my mind would race, and I'd feel like I was crawling out of my own skin. It wasn't just a habit; it was a need.

For those who don't know what addiction feels like... it's OVERWHELMING! On a personal level, it means you've lost control of every aspect of your life. Your only goal is to get your next drink and make sure you have enough alcohol to make it through the night until the liquor store opens again in the morning. By this point in your alcoholic journey, your body is so chemically dependent on alcohol that quitting cold turkey would bring on severe withdrawal symptoms.

One of the saddest things about my alcohol addiction is the way it has affected my family and our relationships. Because of that, I often found myself in situations that were embarrassing, and rather than facing the truth, I would turn to a lie to explain what was going on. But lies build on lies. I had to keep my stories straight, which became exhausting, difficult, and humiliating. Losing my family's trust was what hurt the most. My sons, my grandchildren, my sister. Actually, I know it did. Even though they were gracious enough to still speak to me despite not being able to trust me, I was so grateful.

I am currently sober, and I count each and every day as a blessing. A blessing to be alive and a blessing to have the chance to earn back my family's trust and respect. I know I will be working on this for the rest of my life.

Do I regret everything I've done over the years while living through my alcoholism? Yes. Most definitely. There are no words to fully describe the humiliation, embarrassment, and self-disgust that come with being an alcoholic and an addict. But finally being able to admit, out loud, that I am an alcoholic has been emotionally freeing in ways I never expected. Now, I hold myself accountable each day. Every night, I text a picture of my breathalyzer result to my kids. It not only keeps me accountable but also gives them peace of mind.

When my son told me he was writing a book on this topic and asked if I wanted to share my perspective on how alcohol has shaped my life for the past forty years, I said yes immediately, without hesitation. Because if sharing my experience can open up even one conversation between an addict and their family, then it's worth it.

I hope that by sharing even a small part of my journey, I can help bridge the gap between alcoholics and their loved ones. Open, honest communication is the first step to rebuilding trust. It won't happen overnight, but...it can happen.

Finally, if you are dealing with a loved one's addiction, please know this: They want your trust. They want an open, honest line of communication with you. Those things can change not only their life but yours as well.

So if you are hesitating on whether or not to reach out, do it. If you have been waiting for the right moment to have that hard conversation, don't wait any longer. Change might start with that one honest conversation, but more often, it takes many. And even when it feels like nothing is changing, know that with every conversation, you are making an impact. You just don't see it yet.

Chapter 1

The Normal That Wasn't

Childhood has a way of convincing us that whatever we grow up with is normal. It's only later, when cracks start to show in our adult lives, that we begin to question the foundation we assumed was solid.

I used to think it was normal to feel anxious anytime someone raised their voice, muttered "God dammit" under their breath, shot a mean look across the room, or pressured me to rush through something just so I wouldn't hassle them. I thought it was normal for a small argument to turn into a full-blown ordeal—yelling that started in front of me and carried on behind closed doors, mean looks that said more than words ever could, and apologies that never came straight from the source, only filtered through someone else.

But as an adult, I realized I wasn't just reacting to the moment—I was reliving years of tension at home that had wired me to expect the worst—reading danger into every sigh, every slammed drawer, every change in someone's voice—while everyone else just saw a bad mood and moved on.

I have an embarrassing confession to make. I didn't know my parents were alcoholics or that I had grown up in an alcoholic home until I was nearly 20 years old. In fact, I didn't fully grasp this until my mid-twenties, when patterns in my friendships, relationships with acquaintances and coworkers, and romantic partners repeatedly revealed signs of dysfunction.

Simple things—like lacking self-awareness or struggling to recognize others' needs—became evident in my behavior. I would often prioritize my own needs over theirs. I struggled to relate to others, especially love interests, whose perspectives and social experiences were very different from mine.

For instance, people who grow up in stable homes—where parents are emotionally available and model how to treat others—tend to enter adulthood with a level of emotional maturity that I lacked. Growing up in an environment clouded by chronic alcoholism—and the instability, anger, and emotional neglect that come with it—stunts that growth in ways that are subtle but profound.

There were many moments throughout my youth and young adulthood when I witnessed what others considered "normal" and felt disconnected from it. Instances of parents dressing their child for graduation and cheering as they walked the stage, coworkers celebrating promotions with potlucks, or couples having a joyful, well-deserved date night.

Watching these moments felt like observing another world I wasn't part of. Why did I feel so detached from the love, accomplishment, and joy these events are supposed to bring?

Even in good moments, I struggled to feel like I deserved them. The effects of living around alcoholism were so pervasive that they left me feeling undeserving and unable to fully embrace the happiness in front of me. The constant drunken criticism, harsh words, and lack of affirmation led me to internalize the belief that I was not good enough. I thought, "If I'm not enough to make them love me or change for me, then I must not deserve love at all."

Moving away from home at nineteen, the cracks in my foundation became harder to ignore. Approval-seeking, isolation, impulsive behavior, and difficulty navigating relationships all began surfacing in ways I couldn't yet understand. I often needed constant validation, and when friends or partners didn't give it exactly when I expected, I spiraled into emotional turmoil.

I withdrew from people even as I craved their closeness, and sought quick hits of reassurance through compliments or reactions on social media. Romantic partners probably bore the worst of it. I struggled to give them space, struggled to believe they could love me and still want time apart. I couldn't understand why someone I loved wouldn't want to spend every moment with me.

When you're raised in an alcoholic home, you don't really have a frame of reference for what's healthy or stable. You assume your life mirrors everyone else's—that every family moves through moods like storms, that tension and unpredictability are just part of growing up. You might not even recognize it as dysfunction at the time. You're groomed to believe it's normal, even when something deep inside you knows it shouldn't be.

Jeremy Allen Damours

An alcoholic isn't just someone who drinks—it's someone driven toward drinking, even as it wrecks their relationships, their health, and everything they care about. Clinically, it's called Alcohol Use Disorder—shaped by craving, needing more to feel the same effects, struggling to stop, and drinking even when it hurts them or the people around them. But definitions aside, the reality is harsher: alcohol comes first—and everyone else comes second.

And it runs even deeper than that—because for many alcoholics, the choice isn't as simple as willpower or good intentions. Alcoholism is a devastating disease—one that takes hold of their lives in ways most people on the outside don't fully understand. Some manage to function for a while, holding steady jobs, only to retreat into nightly drinking that pushes family and stability into the background.

Others can't hold jobs at all, trapped in a cycle of constant drinking. Either way, emotional volatility—like mood swings, neglect, and deepening instability—becomes part of daily life for everyone around them.

For children, this instability becomes the backdrop of their normal. Growing up in a home where late-night parties, missed family events, or broken promises were part of everyday life made trust and security hard to establish. That emotional unavailability from parents leaves a lasting void.

If given a choice, I believe many alcoholics would wish to never experience cravings again. In moments of clarity, they recognize their problem but find themselves too weak to resist the pull of the bottle.

Dear Red Straw

Alcoholism is a chronic, lifelong disease that they must fight every single day.

But even so, the ones who love them are fighting too—fighting to stay whole in the wreckage that drinking leaves behind. And long after the alcoholic's battle fades into the background, survivors are still carrying the pieces.

Jeremy Allen Damours

Some of my earliest memories go as far back as when I was three years old. I know because when I'd tell my mom about them later, she'd listen in disbelief, swearing I couldn't have been more than three at the time. Thinking back now, it feels like I've split those early years—three to seven—into two different worlds: the normal-looking days, and the strange, chaotic nights.

In the daylight, our life could almost pass for ordinary. My parents kept the house clean; my dad left early in the mornings for 10- to 12-hour shifts, and my mom stayed home, juggling us and a crowd of other kids she babysat to make ends meet. She held a consistent routine of changing diapers, preparing meals, and scolding us when we misbehaved.

There was Harlan, a red-haired, chubby boy, who often hurt the other children without meaning to. Harmony, quiet and reserved, always off in a corner picking her nose. And Andrew, forever sneezing strings of mucous across the table, making the rest of us scream, "Ew!" as we tried to eat our breakfast.

As chaotic as those moments were, they're some of the most normal memories I have from childhood.

But normalcy faded as evening came. Once my parents were off work, the alcohol would emerge. With each passing hour, my brothers and I would watch as their movements grew sluggish, their speech slurred, and my dad's emotions became volatile. While I didn't understand it at the time, those nights planted a growing sense of uncertainty in me.

My mother, usually apologetic and sensitive, would shower us with hugs and declarations of love, but the way she repeated herself—over and over, losing track of her own words—left me feeling oddly insecure. My father was the opposite. While he occasionally showed affection, he mostly ranted—angrily and endlessly—about work and perceived betrayals.

Like my mother, he repeated himself too, but where her words blurred into desperate affection, his would bumble out at first—rambling, looping, almost tripping over themselves. Then, for reasons I could never understand, the anger would build anyway. We could sit there saying nothing at all, doing nothing wrong, and somehow his voice would still get louder, his words sharper, like he was arguing against someone only he could see.

Once, he was so enraged that my brother and I had eaten the pieces of ham and croutons off his salad that he clenched his teeth, a line of spit clinging to his chin as he seethed, and slammed his fists on the table, yelling, "God dammit, where the hell did my ham go?!"

I felt scared that I had upset him, but at the time, I didn't realize how far from normal his reaction really was. I knew, deep down, that we shouldn't have been picking at food that wasn't ours.

Earlier that evening, my mom had placed two salads on the table while my dad was frying codfish, and she had walked away. Hungry and restless, my brother and I thought it would be funny to sneak a few bites off one of the salads. We didn't know whose it was—there were no names, no way to tell.

We were only seven or eight years old, too immature to think through the consequences, but we also didn't expect any real punishment beyond maybe a mild scolding. Instead, after my dad erupted, we panicked and hid behind the couch, hoping to escape his anger.

We thought the worst was over. We were wrong.

Earlier in the night, my mom had loosened the cap on the salad dressing so my dad could easily pour it onto his plate. But she must have forgotten that he had a habit of violently shaking condiment bottles before opening them, trying to force the contents to the top.

Still seething, my dad grabbed the bottle and began shaking it hard, not realizing the lid was barely on. Salad dressing flew everywhere—across his shirt, into his hair, all over the table and the floor, even splattering the couch where we crouched, frozen in fear.

"Goddamn it!" he roared, cursing and slamming the bottle down.

His rage was so palpable that I stayed hidden as long as I could, praying he was too drunk to stumble over and find us. These were the moments where the seeds of fear were planted that one day his anger would escalate to something truly dangerous.

By then, we were living in Alaska—thousands of miles away from family in Arizona.

We had moved when I was seven, chasing what my parents framed as a new adventure—snow, wilderness, a fresh start. At the time, I didn't fully grasp what this meant, but I remember feeling a mix of excitement and apprehension.

What I didn't understand was how much this move would isolate us from the extended family we had relied on for even a semblance of normalcy. Suddenly, there would be no more visits to see our grandparents, aunts, uncles, or cousins. We would be all alone—without family nearby.

Years later, my mom explained the real reason behind the move: my dad had lost his trucking job, our main source of income, after failing a random drug test at work. Alaska was supposed to be a chance for a fresh start—a place to get sober and away from the hard drugs.

But what actually happened was the opposite. My parents didn't get sober. They replaced drugs with more drinking—and only sank deeper once the drugs were gone. As is often the case with addicts, they shifted their dependency rather than overcoming it. And the more they drank, the more unpredictable everything at home became.

Alaska turned out to be a whole new world for us kids. Seeing snow for the first time was magical. We'd sled down the hills around our home, bust icicles on the rooftops, and drink lots of hot chocolate. One time, we even went ice fishing on Birch Lake and caught a ton of fish.

It was a far cry from the scorching heat and desert landscapes we'd left behind in Arizona. Summers in Alaska had their own kind of magic—bike rides through the valleys, building hideaway forts in the forests, and staying up all night to play outside because the sun never set.

But as time passed, I realized the move was less about creating a new life and more about escaping the watchful eye of extended family. With no family around to hold them accountable, my parents indulged in their vices without restraint. Drinking started earlier in the day. Arguments became more routine and complicated.

Nights stretched on longer, with my parents staying up drinking and stirring up drama, while everything outside our home felt like another world— one we could see but weren't part of anymore, locked out without ever knowing why. Alaska wasn't a new beginning. It was a retreat into deeper dysfunction.

As we grew older, my brothers and I wanted to experience more of life—to attend events, meet friends, and feel something outside the walls of our home. It wasn't about independence; we were still just kids, wanting the simple things other kids had—birthday parties, school dances, sleepovers, afternoons at friends' houses without always feeling rushed, limited, or like we were asking for too much.

But for my parents, these outings were always overshadowed by their need for alcohol. Every trip or activity had an underlying urgency, a clock ticking toward the moment they could get back home and drink. No matter how much we looked forward to something, it always ended up a footnote to the real event: getting back to the bottle.

Dear Red Straw

After a while, it was hard to believe anything we looked forward to would actually feel the way it was supposed to.

My high school graduation was supposed to be one of those big moments. It was supposed to be a milestone—a moment to celebrate years of hard work and the beginning of a new chapter in my life.

When the ceremony started, we sat in rows near the front of the stage, waiting for our names to be called. I could feel the energy buzzing around me. Families behind us were erupting into cheers, laughter, and pride. Even though none of us held diplomas yet, my classmates had something I couldn't seem to touch: the tangible love and excitement of their families.

I sat there, stiff in my wrinkled robe, trying not to fidget with the tassel I couldn't figure out how to pin. My white sneakers were cracked and worn, a sharp contrast to the polished black leather dress shoes so many of the others wore. I felt a quiet embarrassment settle in. I hadn't known to ask for better shoes—or maybe I hadn't felt like I could. Either way, I showed up the best I could, even if it didn't quite feel like enough.

When I struggled with my cap, a teacher I didn't know walked over, adjusted it for me, and patted down my robe as if trying to iron out more than just wrinkles. For a moment, her steady hands quieted the unease I had carried with me all night. It was just a small moment, but for a few seconds, it felt like someone actually saw me.

Jeremy Allen Damours

When my row was called, we filed backstage, our shoes clicking against the floor, each step pulling us closer to the black curtain—the thin veil between childhood and everything that came next. After tonight, we were expected to step into the world as adults: some heading off to college, others straight into work, all of us somehow expected to figure it out. My heart was pounding. I told myself to be proud.

But when my name was finally called and I stepped into the lights, I didn't hear a single familiar voice—just silence pressing down from the crowd. I barely breathed. I just kept moving.

I kept moving because I had to. Because I still believed the celebration would come afterward—that somehow, outside those walls, things would be different.

I was already picturing it—taking pictures with my family, soaking in the joy of the occasion. More than anything, I was hopeful—hopeful that my parents, especially my dad, would not just stand for pictures, but be proud. I could almost see it in my mind: him standing outside on the sidewalk, the afternoon sun warming his face, the breeze lifting his dark hair.

I pictured a grin so wide it didn't need words to show how proud he was—that I could feel it. I saw him looking at me not just as his son, but as proof that some of the mistakes he had made—dropping out of high school, struggling to find his footing—had somehow been redeemed through me. In that moment, I wanted to be his pride, his joy, his shining star.

Dear Red Straw

But that moment never came. My dad, impatient and restless, insisted we leave almost immediately. He couldn't bear to stay away from his alcohol any longer.

What should have been a day of pride and happiness was cut short by the ever-present pull of addiction. That day became a symbol of how alcoholism robbed us of so many experiences. Even the most precious milestones were overshadowed by their drinking, leaving me with memories colored more by disappointment than by joy.

Sometimes, my mom's drinking made it hard to tell where parent ended and friend began. One night when I was around thirteen, she handed my brothers and me White Russians—Kahlua and milk over ice—and smiled like it was just another part of growing up. What kid would say no to something that tasted more like dessert and felt like being let in on a secret? We'd have one drink, then maybe another after she went to bed.

At the time, it felt harmless—just another way the lines between childhood and adulthood kept getting stretched, making it seem normal.

I've thought about it a lot over the years. Why would a mother make alcoholic drinks for her kids? I think it was her way of making her own drinking feel normal—less wrong. If we drank too, then it wasn't just her bad habit anymore. Maybe it even felt like bonding to her. But what she didn't see was how much it chipped away at our innocence, little by little.

At the time, it felt exciting, even special, to be included in what seemed like an adult privilege. But as I grew older, I realized it was another way her addiction seeped into our lives, shaping our understanding of what was normal and leaving behind confusion and emotional scars.

"Just so you know, I will always love your mother more than I love you." Those words, spoken by my father more than once, stung me deeply. Even now, they echo in my mind, a great source of pain and confusion.

I can still remember how it felt to hear him say those words. It was like when I was first learning to ride a bike—feeling safe because I thought someone was holding on. But then the hand let go, and I was on my own, wobbling into the unknown. When I fell and scraped my knees, the sense of safety vanished, replaced by pain and confusion.

That's what it felt like when my dad said he loved my mom more than me.

It wasn't just what he said—it was what it broke inside me.

Deep down, I know my dad loved us. But those words made me question how deep that love went. Was it just the alcohol talking? Or did he mean it? His face, even in his drunken state, was so serious, so lucid in those moments. Fathers are supposed to love their children no matter what—and make them feel safe in that love. Hearing him say otherwise left a wound that never fully healed.

Dear Red Straw

That wound—the words my father spoke—didn't just hurt in the moment. They shaped my sense of what was normal and planted a quiet doubt about my worth that I carried with me into adulthood.

As children, our parents' opinions hold immense weight. When parents share their thoughts openly and constructively, they create a safe space for reflection, growth, and dialogue. Over time, this foundation helps us process the opinions of others more constructively, preparing us for healthy relationships. However, when those opinions are delivered in hurtful or destructive ways, they have the opposite effect.

When my dad convincingly told me he would always love my mother more than me, he shattered that safe space. Instead of fostering connection, his words created emotional—and even physical—barriers between us. I felt unwanted and unloved. Because I believed him, those barriers didn't just exist between us; they began to extend to others in my life as well.

Sometimes, it felt easier to love strangers than to love my own family. Showing love to the people closest to me—both emotionally and physically—felt awkward, foreign, and risky.

As I grew older and began dating, that fear didn't go away—it only intensified. The closer I felt to someone, the harder it became to show affection. Though I could feel love deeply, I often felt too vulnerable to express it—like showing it would leave me exposed and unprotected. That fear kept my feelings bottled up, and eventually, it took a toll on the people I cared about most.

That fear had been planted long before I ever tried to love anyone.

By the time I was six years old, I was so shy that it was incredibly painful to even walk by teachers and students at school. I don't know why I was so shy or how I became that way at such a young age. I just knew it affected everything—even the way my teachers saw me.

My kindergarten teacher convinced my parents to hold my twin brother and me back a year because our shyness was so severe that it was preventing us from making healthy friendships. To help us along in our social development, they believed another year in kindergarten would better prepare us for the rest of our school careers.

My brother and I were also placed in speech therapy because of a speech impediment. We couldn't pronounce the 'r' sound correctly. Our speech teacher, who also had a severe speech impediment herself, worked hard to help us, though it oftentimes made the lessons more challenging to follow. In hindsight, the whole situation feels like a snapshot of my childhood: a well-meaning attempt to create normalcy in a world full of contradictions.

It's these contradictions that stand out most vividly when I think about my childhood—like a compass that points in two directions at once. Our speech teacher, working diligently to teach others to speak clearly while struggling with her own impediment, became one of the clearest reflections of that tension.

In so many ways, her struggle to fulfill that role felt like a reflection of my parents' efforts to create normalcy in a home shaped by the chaos of alcoholism. Both were noble attempts at making something whole out of broken pieces, though neither could completely overcome the challenges they faced.

Not every memory from that time is painful—some still hold a flicker of laughter. Years later, I've come to appreciate the strange irony of having a speech teacher whose own struggles spilled into the classroom. Sometimes, the strange sounds she made would send my brother and me into fits of laughter—not out of cruelty, but because we couldn't help finding it funny as kids.

After enough incidents of frustrating—and probably insulting—her, she called our mother in for a conference. She wanted to lecture us in front of our mom about how disrespectful we were being by laughing during speech therapy. I don't know if she realized that we were laughing at her speech impediment or if she just thought we were being rambunctious boys. Either way, she got our mom involved.

I distinctly remember my brother and me walking down the empty outdoor corridor to the school's main office after classes had started that morning, following our mom as she marched in front of us.

Jeremy Allen Damours

I'll never forget the look on my mother's face when our speech teacher introduced herself and began explaining our bad behavior. She said her biggest issue with us was how we laughed all the time and couldn't stay serious long enough to finish our speech therapy exercises.

It didn't take long before my mother became visibly distracted by the teacher's own speech impediment. Eventually, she couldn't hold it in any longer and began laughing hysterically.

I suspect the speech teacher realized why my mother was laughing, but I don't remember her addressing it in the moment. My mother tried as hard as she could to hold back her laughter, and sometimes she managed, but the majority of the time she just couldn't.

On the walk home after the meeting, my mom surprised us by saying we could skip the rest of the school day. She laughed harder than I'd ever seen her laugh, apologizing between fits of giggles for being so tough on us. She said she finally understood why we couldn't stop laughing during speech therapy.

That was one of the happiest times I remember with my mother growing up—seeing her happy, smiling, and being childlike herself. It was a rare instance when she came down to our level, when I felt like she truly understood us and our predicaments. That shared laughter proved that even in the midst of dysfunction, we could find ways to connect and understand each other.

Humor didn't erase the chaos, but it gave us fleeting glimpses where life felt lighter and more

Dear Red Straw

bearable. Experiences like these reminded me that healing doesn't happen all at once—it unfolds in small, human exchanges where we find each other again. Even in a life shaped by struggle, connection can spark understanding and keep the light alive, one step at a time.

Jeremy Allen Damours

As I get older, I see more clearly how deeply my childhood experiences shaped my understanding of the world—and my place in it. The chaos I grew up in defined so much of what I thought was normal, but I've learned it doesn't have to define my tomorrow. Growth begins when we recognize the patterns that no longer serve us—and find the courage to rewrite them.

Breaking unhealthy cycles isn't easy. It takes a lot of introspection, honesty, and a willingness to face the past while imagining a better way forward. For me, it's meant acknowledging the wounds I carried, breaking down the walls I built, and learning to believe in the possibility of balance and connection. Every small step toward healing has shown me that it's possible to grow into a healthier, more whole version of myself.

The pain of the past may never fully disappear, but it doesn't have to dictate who we become. Growth means making the choice, day by day, to build a life that reflects not where we've been, but where we want to go.

Dear Red Straw

Dear Mom and Dad,

I thought this letter would be full of anger. Maybe it should be. But it's not. At least, not yet.

I've spent so many years looking back, picking apart memories, trying to make sense of it all. But I can't seem to do that anymore. There's nothing left to untangle. The only thing I can do is accept it.

I've seen what anger does to a person. When my marriage fell apart and I was left raising the boys alone, I was furious. The kind of anger that crawls under your skin and settles in your bones. I didn't know how I was going to survive— how I'd work, take care of them, or have anything that resembled a life at 25. I hated her for leaving me like that. That rage hollowed me out, left me drowning in depression. There were days when I thought I couldn't take it anymore. But eventually, I let it go. Not for her. For me. For the boys.

That's probably why I'm not angry at you anymore. Because I know now that *holding onto it would only keep me stuck in a place I now refuse to live in.*

But just because I'm not angry doesn't mean I've made peace with what happened. I don't believe you ever meant to hurt me. But I also don't think you cared enough to stop.

It angers me that every family trip felt rushed because you couldn't wait to get back home and drink. I'm embarrassed about the way I had to sit in silence while friends and relatives gave each other those looks, like they saw something wrong with you that I hadn't figured out yet. And there was something wrong. I had you figured out. I just didn't have the words for it. But they definitely knew.

I'm pissed about the way I lost you both to alcohol, every single day. In the mornings, you were there. But by the afternoon? You were gone. And Dad, you'd get meaner as the night went on, spitting words like venom, yelling at me for things I didn't even understand. You both put so much on me that no kid should ever have to carry. And the worst part? I thought it was normal.

Dear Red Straw

I thought every family was like this. I thought every house had a liquor cabinet that never ran dry. I thought everybody's parents drank all the time. I thought every family lived in separate corners of the same home, avoiding each other, except when the alcohol took over and made you loud, affectionate, or cruel. I thought this was just how families worked.

Until that Christmas.

The year Josh and I went to Montana to visit Jesse's family.

That was the first time I saw what normal actually looked like.

Jesse's parents talked to us. Not small talk. Not passing comments in between sips of a drink. They asked questions and waited for real answers without interrupting. They wanted to know what we were into, what we wanted to be when we grew up. And when we answered, they actually listened. That alone felt foreign.

And then there was Jesse. She hugged her parents, and they hugged her back—not the way drunk people hug, not the way you'd cling to me, Mom, squeezing tight, apologizing for nothing and everything at the same time. And Dad, the only time you ever hugged me was when you were drunk, your eyes glossed over, your mind racing with distant thoughts. I should have just hugged the bottle, it would have felt just as genuine.

No, this was different. It was normal.

I remember watching them, feeling like an outsider, like I was witnessing something I wasn't supposed to see. Their closeness actually made me feel uncomfortable. But more than anything, I remember being jealous.

I wanted that.

And when I had to go back home without it, I was angry all over again.

That was the first time I saw it—clear as day. We weren't normal. We never had been

I get it now. You were addicts. And in a lot of ways, I know you couldn't control it.

Dear Red Straw

But that doesn't mean I'm giving you an excuse.

I hope you found whatever it was you were chasing at the bottom of those bottles. Even if it came at the cost of us.

But I need you to know—I'm walking away from it now.

And I'm not picking it up again.

CHAPTER 2

TRAPPED ON EDGE

Ten years into my nursing career, burnout from long hours and patient care pushed me to explore a completely different path: mortuary science. It was a respect that began when my one-year-old son, Nathaniel, passed away from Menkes disease. I was just nineteen years old. If a mortuary science program had been available in Alaska, I would have pursued a career in funeral service.

Grant was the one who helped us through the funeral arrangements. He looked young—too young, almost—to own a funeral home with his wife. He spoke softly, almost in a whisper, and carried himself with a humble, respectful spirit. He made me feel a little less alone—and at that point in my life, that small sense of comfort meant everything.

Back then, funeral announcements were published in the local newspaper. The internet wasn't widely used yet for things like that, and in a small town like ours, everybody read the paper. The day Nathaniel's announcement was supposed to run, it wasn't there. Grant called us as soon as he realized the mistake he had made. He was deeply apologetic and arranged for the announcement to be placed immediately, making sure it appeared the very next day—the morning of Nathaniel's funeral.

Some later told us they saw the announcement that morning and rushed over, just barely making it in time. I should have been upset, but I was too numb. I couldn't process things. In a way, Grant's honesty and handling of it softened the edges of the moment, and that meant far more to me than getting everything right.

To make up for the mistake, he gave us a discount on the modest cardboard casket my family and I could barely afford. It was a welcomed act of kindness. I'd grown up in a world that often felt one step away from breaking—but in that moment, someone outside our chaos tried to ease the pressure. It was a small thing, but it stayed with me—maybe because so little else did.

I'll never forget the day we buried Nathaniel.

It was a beautiful Alaskan spring day—the kind that still feels like winter if you're standing in the shade. The last of the snow had melted into the dirt, and you could smell the moisture rising up as the ground finished thawing. Birds sang like they were waking the world up again, and the trees were just beginning to blush with new leaves, tiny bursts of green against the gray branches.

Nathaniel's tiny casket sat next to his freshly dug grave, perched so neatly beside a hole cut into the earth with such sharp, perfect corners. I remember sitting there in silence, taking it all in—the smell of the damp soil, the light breeze, the sound of birdsong layered over the sound of my own despair.

Dear Red Straw

I noticed who was there. My aunt and uncle, Dave and Connie, had come. So had the pastor who was helping with the service, along with a few members of his family, and some friends and relatives of ours.

But there were also faces missing. The pastor had warned me in advance not to take it personally—said people don't like attending funerals, and even fewer stay for burials. I didn't take it personally. If anything, I felt grateful for every person who came and stayed, who didn't look away.

While the pastor spoke, I kept my eyes locked on the casket, not hearing most of what he said. All I could think was, "I want to see him again. I need to see him again."

People were starting to walk away, but I couldn't do it. I stood there, staring at his casket, fighting the growing panic in my soul. I knew that if I didn't look inside one last time—if I didn't see that Nathaniel was really there—I'd always carry a quiet fear that maybe he wasn't.

That maybe, in some unimaginable way, I had gotten it wrong. It sounds irrational, but I needed to know, deep in my heart, that my baby boy would always be in that spot, resting beneath my feet whenever I came to visit.

Grant quietly explained that he wasn't supposed to open the casket outdoors. But when he saw the desperation in my eyes, he didn't hesitate. He lifted the lid just enough for me to see Nathaniel one last time.

I'll never forget what he did for me, breaking whatever rules he needed to. When I nodded, he gently closed the casket again, and I stood there for hours and watched as the gravediggers buried my son.

Watching the earth cascade over Nathaniel's casket left an imprint on my heart I couldn't fully understand at the time. It wasn't just the finality of death that stayed with me—it was the quiet strength of those who helped me through it.

I've always believed that funeral directors do sacred work—the kind that holds families together when their world is falling apart. They help carry the weight of grief, creating space for love, loss, and memory to coexist with dignity. As much as I felt drawn to that path, it simply wasn't possible at the time—not in the way I was just beginning to imagine. So I turned to nursing, and built a life around caring for the living instead.

But years later, while living in Texas, the pull toward that old dream came back. This time, I had the opportunity I didn't have before. So I enrolled in a funeral directing program, finally giving myself the chance to pursue what I'd once thought was out of reach.

Being in a classroom again after all those years felt surprisingly good, surrounded by students who, in many ways, reminded me of a younger version of myself—eager, curious, trying to make sense of the work ahead. I took it seriously. This wasn't just a career change; it felt like a return to something unfinished.

Most days were quiet, routine. We studied theory, ethics, the technical details of the profession.

Then one day, something felt off.

Dear Red Straw

I was sitting in class when I had a sudden, unshakable feeling that something was about to go wrong. Everything around me seemed normal—students listening, the professor mid-lecture—but the ambient noise just instantly vanished. It was like someone hit mute on everything except his voice.

All I could hear was him speaking. His words felt sharp, almost disconnected from the rest of the room. And at the same time, a thick pressure started building around my head. It wasn't pain exactly—it was more like something was closing in, and my brain was scrambling to make sense of it.

I knew something was wrong. I didn't know what it was yet, but my body already had the message. My mind was just trying to catch up.

"A student just collapsed on the floor!" yelled a frantically shaking voice from behind me.

I was already on my feet before I knew what I was doing. My body had moved first.

I found her slumped on the floor, just starting to come to. I knelt beside her, heart racing, trying to figure out what was happening.

"Do you have any medical problems?"

"No."

"Have you eaten today?"

"Not since yesterday. I've been stressed. Studying. I forgot."

Someone nearby grabbed a sugary drink and handed it to me. I held it out as she took slow sips while her breathing steadied. The color started to return to her face, and her eyes relaxed. As the panic faded, something in me eased too—like we'd both come down from a place we didn't expect to be.

I sat there for a moment, trying to understand how I'd known before I saw anything. It didn't make sense—but it did. It wasn't surprising, just something my body had already decided. Later, I couldn't stop thinking about it—how I moved before I even knew what I was doing. It didn't feel like a choice. It felt like instinct.

There are moments when your body knows before your mind can catch up. How my body just moved without asking permission.

When you're always carrying tension just beneath the surface, you start picking up on small flickers: a tone of voice, the way someone breathes, the silence between words. You learn to notice the smallest details, not out of curiosity, but because you're always gearing up for impact. You're not just tuning into the room—you're scoping it, constantly. Not for fun. For survival. You become someone who's always listening for the thing that hasn't happened yet.

That instinct didn't come out of nowhere. I'd spent years living in a house where friction drifted in the air long before anyone raised their voice. My body learned early to expect that quiet wasn't always safe—and that stillness could be just as dangerous.

My father was a kind man during the day, when work forced him to stay sober. But by late afternoon, once the hours were his own again, the cracks would

Dear Red Straw

start to show. The smallest things—me taking too long in the shower, my brothers misplacing something in the kitchen, my mother forgetting to shut a cabinet door—could set him off. He'd explode out of nowhere, slamming drawers, pounding his fists on the counter, yelling about how no one respected him. He often claimed we were trying to undermine him.

Other times he'd recall the past, digging up old grievances between him and my mother, or inventing new ones that hadn't happened at all. His anger felt like a current running through the house, and we lived in constant fear of being caught in its path. Even the dogs acted differently when he was on edge, their tails tucked low, flinching at sudden sounds—like they were bracing too.

Living under that kind of volatility changes you, even when you don't realize it. I started to believe my worth was tied to how well I could keep my dad calm—and eventually, how well I could keep everyone else happy too.

At school, I avoided confrontation at all costs. I didn't know how to stand up to bullies or hold my ground in arguments, because the first example of conflict I ever knew—my father—always won. There was no reasoning with him, no talking things through. At home, conflict didn't lead to understanding; it led to fear.

And so outside the home, I wasn't prepared to handle it either. I didn't fight back. I'd freeze up, or walk away, just to make it stop. Sometimes that defused the moment, but it never resolved anything—not out there, and definitely not inside me. It left me anxious, ashamed, and questioning of my own strength.

By the time I got my first job as a bagger at a grocery store, the pressure to hold everything together—to stop tension before it started—was already in me. I worked like every shift was a test I couldn't afford to fail. I bent over backward to keep my boss happy, afraid that even a small mistake would turn me into a disappointment.

I went out of my way to be kind to customers, even when they snapped at me over things I couldn't control. Every complaint felt like confirmation that I was the problem. No matter how much I told myself otherwise, each one chipped away at whatever self-worth I had left.

Even with coworkers, I struggled to set boundaries. If someone needed to trade shifts, I'd agree—no matter what it cost me. I could be exhausted, have plans, or desperately need a day to rest—but I'd say yes anyway, because I couldn't bear the thought of disappointing someone.

The idea of saying no made me physically uneasy. It felt risky, like I might lose their approval or set off something I wouldn't know how to handle. My own needs never felt as urgent as keeping the peace. I wasn't just being nice—I was trying to protect myself. And every time I gave in, a small part of me disappeared under someone else's comfort.

What I now realize is that none of it was ever about being nice. It was survival. I spent so long managing other people's comfort that I never really learned how to recognize my own.

I didn't lose myself—I never really got to know who I was to begin with. Unlearning that meant peeling back the parts of me that were built around keeping the peace. That imbalance—living for everyone else at the expense of myself—wasn't just unhealthy. It was the first thing I had to undo before I could even begin to build a life that felt like mine.

Even when I wanted things to change—and started doing the work to change them—I couldn't always turn it off. Some days I could. Some days I couldn't. That constant awareness, that tension in my body, that feeling like something might shift at any second—it was still there.

But over time, I started to notice it wasn't all bad. That same awareness helped me stay sharp. It made me more careful in certain situations, more attuned to what was happening around me. The real work wasn't about getting rid of it. It was learning how to use it without letting it take over.

And in our house, it didn't take much for things to fall apart.

My dad blamed my mom for everything. And I mean everything. And I don't mean typical arguments over chores or parenting.

I mean blaming her when he'd spill his own drink. For dinner not tasting right—even when he was the one who made it. For taking a wrong turn—even though she wasn't the one in the driver's seat. It didn't matter what it was. If he was frustrated, it was her fault.

If his drink didn't taste the way he hoped—"God DAMNIT, Kathy!"

If dinner wasn't seasoned just right—"God DAMNIT, Kathy!"

If he couldn't find something he misplaced, or the remote wasn't where he last left it—"God DAMNIT, Kathy!"

If the dogs got underfoot or one of us ate the last of something—same thing. Same voice. Same rage.

It became a near-daily refrain. And the anger behind it wasn't mild or passing—it was sharp, seething, and impossible to ignore.

"God DAMNIT, Kathy!" wasn't just something my dad yelled—it was his signature. You could see it coming. His face would contort, his jaw would clench, and his teeth would gnash together just before the words erupted. His eyes would narrow in a squint of disgust, and his whole demeanor would shift into something unrecognizable. Then came the outburst: "God DAMNIT, Kathy!"

It was frightening to witness—not just because of his tone, but because of the sheer intensity behind it. And while he didn't lash out physically in those moments, the possibility always lingered. He looked like someone who could, and that thought alone was enough to scare me.

My body would freeze the second he erupted. Sometimes I'd stay completely still, afraid to make a sound. Other times I'd slip out of the room quietly, hoping to disappear before he found a reason to turn on me too.

To protect myself, I got good at reading him—his expressions, his tone, the energy in the room. I could feel his anger coming before he even said a word. It became a kind of survival skill. The better I got at reading him, the more I avoided him.

As a kid, that meant retreating to my room or spending hours outside, anywhere but near him. And when I finally got my driver's license at sixteen, it wasn't just freedom—it was escape. That license wasn't a milestone for me. It was a lifeline.

At school, I kept my head down. I followed the rules, avoided the spotlight, and stayed far away from anything that felt like confrontation. I didn't raise my hand in class. I didn't join teams or clubs. I tried to overachieve just enough to avoid criticism, but never enough to stand out.

And when someone crossed a line with me, I said nothing. I didn't know how. Even the smallest tension at school felt bigger than me—like it would crush me if I pushed back.

Being alert all the time didn't just condition me to read people—to pick up on unease, to sense what others needed before they said a word. It made me more empathetic. It also made me afraid—afraid of saying the wrong thing, of being too much, of being seen at all. It kept me in the corners of my own life.

That same sensitivity pulled me toward the underdogs. The kids who didn't fit in. The ones who were awkward, shy, or always left out. I saw myself in them, because I was one of them. I was the nerd. The quiet kid. The one who stayed invisible on purpose.

I'll never forget one day in seventh or eighth grade—English class, I think—when one of the popular kids came up to me after class. I didn't know him. I hadn't done anything that stood out that day. But he pulled me aside, away from his friends, and said, "You'd be a really cool guy if you just opened up and talked more."

That moment stopped me. It was the first time I realized that even when I was working so hard to go unseen, I was still seen. I thought nobody noticed me—but somebody did.

And if he noticed me, maybe others did too. That thought felt strange, a little scary. But also kind of freeing. Maybe I could matter to people. Maybe I already did.

Dear Red Straw

Some of the things that helped me survive back then started to hurt me later. I was so focused on everyone else—what they needed, what they might say or do—that I wasn't paying attention to myself.

Finding the balance between caring and protecting myself wasn't easy. But noticing how off it all felt—that was the first real step toward something better.

And just because I noticed it didn't mean I knew how to change it.

Not being able to let my guard down didn't just make me brace for conflict—it made me alert to everything. That edge followed me into everyday life, where I found myself overthinking every look, every shift in tone.

I was always trying to figure out what people really meant, if they were upset, if I'd done something wrong. It left me tangled in guilt, self-doubt, and second-guessing.

That fear—of doing something wrong, asking for too much, or being seen the wrong way—was buried deep. I didn't understand it then, but even in third grade, I was already learning to hold myself back.

Ms. Maxwell was my third grade teacher. She was older, a little rough around the edges, and cared a lot about her students. She took her job seriously. She was tough on us, but kind at the same time—a kind of maternal toughness, like we were her own kids.

Jeremy Allen Damours

That toughness stood out even more the day she told the class—completely out of nowhere, totally unexpected, because who would've thought—that her husband had died years earlier from a rabies infection.

That story stuck with me. Rabies felt like something from another time—not something that happened to people anymore. I didn't fully understand what it was, but the image I formed in my head was terrifying. I imagined her husband foaming at the mouth, maybe even turning into some kind of wild forest creature.

It sounded so painful and horrifying that, for a while, I was afraid to go out for recess, worried a rabid animal would crawl out of the woods behind our school and attack me.

Around the same time Ms. Maxwell told us that story, I started noticing that my pudding cup kept disappearing from my lunchbox. Every day, when I'd take out my sandwich, chips, and Capri Sun—the pudding, which I always saved for last—would be missing. At first, I thought I'd forgotten to pack it. But when it happened again—and then again—I started to suspect someone was stealing it.

At home, I double-checked the pudding count. It was definitely going in the lunchbox. Which meant there was a problem: a pudding bandit in the classroom.

After the third incident, my mom called Ms. Maxwell to report the missing pudding cups and see if anything could be done. When I found out she'd gotten Ms. Maxwell involved, I felt an unexpected wave of guilt. It seemed like such a small thing to make a fuss over. I felt like my problem wasn't big enough to matter—like I was just making trouble. That I shouldn't be bothering anyone with it.

And now that it was out in the open, Ms. Maxwell had to come up with a creative plan to catch the thief.

She told my mom to mark the bottom of the pudding cups with a black checkmark. Then, at lunchtime, she'd casually walk around the room to see if anyone else had one with the same mark.

It wasn't long before the pudding bandit struck again—and Ms. Maxwell carried out her plan as promised. As we ate lunch at our desks, she strolled past each student, pausing just long enough to see if they had a pudding cup. When she got to Richard—a classmate I couldn't stand because he was a bully—he was eating a vanilla pudding. Ms. Maxwell asked to see the bottom, and there it was: a black checkmark. I'll never forget the way she turned around and gave me a knowing smile from across the room. She'd caught him.

Turned out Richard had been sneaking into the classroom during recess, going through my cubby, and slipping the pudding into his own lunch. I was relieved his little crime spree had finally come to a screeching halt. And I was grateful to Ms. Maxwell—for catching him, and for showing me that even something as small as a pudding cup was worth standing up for.

The guilt I felt wasn't really about the pudding. There was something else underneath it. It was about feeling exposed—taking up space in someone else's world without knowing if they wanted me there. It was trying not to need anything, so even something small felt like a lot to ask. At home, I learned to figure things out quietly so no one exploded. So at school, asking for help didn't feel like a right. It felt like the same kind of risk.

There was another thing about Ms. Maxwell that, years later, made me think about my struggle with being seen—and how I processed the world around me. Being anxious all the time had trained me to read deeply into my parents. That's what kept me safe at home. I learned to watch for changes in their face or mood—especially with my dad.

But away from the house, it didn't work the same way. I tried to read other people like I read my parents, without knowing their full backstory. Without that context, my assumptions were often wrong. I could tell by the way people looked at me—confused, unsure, like we were on two different wavelengths. That lack of connection made me feel out of place. Misunderstood. Like I didn't fit in.

I probably came off as quiet, distant, maybe even too serious. People assumed I didn't care or wasn't paying attention—when really, I was feeling everything. Every little thing. But I didn't know their stories, so I filled in the blanks myself. And that made me seem off to others. The other kids weren't watching the world like I was. They didn't have to.

One afternoon during science hour, Ms. Maxwell had us gather at the front of the classroom for a demonstration. She pulled a red balloon out of her pocket, pursed her lips over the floppy rubber tip, and began to blow it up. With each puff, we watched the

Dear Red Straw

balloon slowly stretch and grow until it looked like it was going to burst.

Just when we thought it would, she stopped, tied the end into a knot, and started telling us about static electricity. To make it more fun, she began talking to the balloon like it was a real person.

As she brought it closer to her face, the static finally pulled it tight against her cheeks, like it had found the perfect spot and didn't want to let go. She began wiggling her cheeks, making silly faces, and begging the balloon to unstick from her skin. The whole class thought it was hilarious. Everyone was laughing.

Everyone except me.

I sat there trying to force a reaction. All I could think was—it's just a balloon. It's not real. How is everyone finding this funny? I felt tense, almost irritated, that no one else seemed to feel the same way I did.

But it really wasn't about the balloon. I didn't know how to let go and enjoy the moment with the other kids. I couldn't stop watching, couldn't stop thinking. I didn't know how to just laugh.

I didn't think anyone had noticed. But Ms. Maxwell did.

Her eyebrows arched slightly as she glanced in my direction and gave a little smirk, as if she was trying to nudge me into laughing along. But the longer she looked at me, the more uncomfortable I became. The guilt started building inside me.

Jeremy Allen Damours

To make her feel better, and to break the building tension, I tried fake laughing just to blend in, but it felt forced and awkward. So I quickly gave up. My mind began spiraling into a mess of emotions—annoyance at the situation, guilt for disappointing Ms. Maxwell, and frustration with myself for caring enough about something that didn't even seem all that important.

The next day was parent-teacher conferences. I remember going with my parents and being told to wait outside the classroom while Ms. Maxwell spoke with them. As I sat there by the door, I overheard her telling them that something was wrong with me. She brought up the balloon activity from the day before—how I didn't laugh or show any emotion like the other kids—and said she found it concerning.

Hearing her say I wasn't normal stung deeply. In my heart, I believed I was normal, and that Ms. Maxwell was mistaken—I just didn't think the activity was funny. But her words made me question myself. The same feelings I'd had during the balloon lesson came rushing back, only worse. I felt humiliated in front of my parents, guilty for not pleasing her, and confused about whether something really was wrong with me.

I didn't just feel out of place—no matter how hard I tried, it felt like I wasn't measuring up.

The truth is, it wasn't just about avoiding conflict. Worrying about how people were reacting—wondering if I was doing something wrong—started shaping how I saw myself. I wasn't just trying to keep the peace. I was trying to be whatever people needed me to be so I wouldn't upset them.

Dear Red Straw

I stopped asking what I needed. I got stuck in this loop of second-guessing everything, feeling guilty for taking up space, and believing that keeping everyone else comfortable was the only way I could be okay.

Jeremy Allen Damours

One of my biggest frustrations growing up was how hard it felt to express what I was really feeling—especially when my mom would ask me if something was wrong. I can barely remember my dad ever asking me that question directly.

If he sensed something was off with one of us, he'd usually ask my mom in private—but only during big, dramatic moments when the tension was too painful to ignore. And the only reason I even knew he asked was because she would eventually tell me. It always felt strange that he couldn't ask me himself—that he filtered his concern through her instead.

If he ever did ask me what was wrong—which was rare—it was only when he was drunk. That annoyed me even more. His empathy felt shallow, fake, like it wasn't really him asking. It was the alcohol talking.

It was the same way with my mom—also the alcohol—but somehow, she was better at fighting through it. She made me feel like there was still some real concern behind that fruity breath. It was a little more believable with her.

I craved their attention, their validation—some sign that what I was going through mattered, even if it was just teenage stuff. But I became more and more afraid of being brushed off. My dad was good at minimizing my feelings, even when he wasn't drinking—always comparing them to other people's bigger problems, or to his own. I felt small.

Dear Red Straw

So I shut down—little by little, year after year. Not being able to talk to my parents about how I felt left me searching elsewhere. I started hoping someone—anyone—outside the house might care enough to ask about me. Maybe a teacher. A friend. Somebody. But I was shy. Scared of being brushed off or made to feel stupid. So I kept it all in. Bottled everything up and carried it around because I didn't know what else to do with it

One night I tried opening up to my dad. He was drunk, of course, and I should've known better. But I was desperate. I needed his advice—even though I knew I wouldn't get it.

I sat on the edge of his bed and poured my heart out. I told him I was only 17, and she was pregnant. I told him how scared I was to become a father. I needed him to listen. To comfort me. To be stern with me. I needed a father's wisdom in that moment. And more than anything, I needed to feel his hand on my shoulder.

He struggled to listen. Struggled to comprehend. His eyes were glazed over, his face stuck in a blank expression that never changed. A hiccup or two slipped out. He could barely sit up, slouched and detached from everything around him.

Then, suddenly, he cut me off. "Do you trust her?" he asked, slurring his words. Before I could answer, he burst into a rant about how much he didn't trust my mother—dragging up old wounds, the infidelities, everything that had gone wrong between them. His voice grew louder. His tone turned meaner. My problem was gone—pushed away by his. I sat there, shrinking. Feeling small. Ashamed for thinking he could meet me in that moment. Foolish for letting myself hope.

I walked away feeling even emptier than before.

That night, he convinced me my feelings didn't matter—and that talking about them was pointless. It would take years to unlearn that, to even begin finding a voice I hadn't yet learned to use.

Dear Red Straw

Being trapped on edge wasn't something I chose—it was something I got good at because I had to. It kept me safe when emotions ran high and things felt unpredictable.

But the habits that helped me get through childhood came with a cost: they left me feeling disconnected from myself, stuck in a cycle of overthinking and doing too much.

The truth is, we don't have to stay stuck in the patterns we learned just to get by. Being on high alert might've helped us back then, but it doesn't have to work the same way now. We can respect what it did to protect us—and still give ourselves permission to live differently now.

Taking back who we are means noticing the old habits that still have a hold on us—like believing our worth depends on keeping the peace, or thinking it's our job to manage how other people feel, even when it costs us.

It means learning to set boundaries—not to push people away, but to protect what we need. And it means finding strength in being honest—realizing that sharing how we feel doesn't make us weak. It makes us human.

As you keep going, remember that growth doesn't happen all at once. It's in the small moments—the ones where you pause, take a breath, and choose to put yourself first. It's when you stop carrying the weight of everyone else's emotions and finally make space for your own.

This shift isn't easy, but it matters. Every time you choose differently, you're building a life where empathy and self-respect can live side by side.

Because reclaiming yourself isn't just about letting go of old habits. It's about learning to live in a way where you feel seen—not just by others, but by yourself. And that's where real healing begins.

Dear Red Straw

Dear Mom and Dad,

I wish you knew—really knew—the pain I felt when Mom left Dad to go to Arizona, trying to escape his drinking and toxicity. It's strange to me because, Mom, while you were running from his drinking, you weren't hell-bent on stopping your own. Maybe you just needed space to think. Maybe you wanted to breathe for a moment without his rants poisoning the air.

When I heard you left without telling Dad, I was relieved. For the first time in my life, I felt hopeful—hopeful that you were choosing something different, that you were finally breaking free. I wanted to believe that this was your chance to start over, to stop drinking, to take your life back. I wanted to believe that maybe, just maybe, I could get my mother back.

But I was wrong.

You went to Arizona, and the drinking never stopped. The only difference was that Dad wasn't there to make it worse, wasn't there to pick fights or fill the air with his drunken rage. But nothing changed. And I had to come to terms with it.

    Still, that wasn't even what hurt me the most.

    Mom, do you remember me telling you how Dad called me every single day, drunk, demanding to know where you were? Do you remember how I told you that no matter how many times I swore I didn't know, he wouldn't believe me? He'd hang up, call other people, and then circle back to me again, slurring threats through the phone—how he was going to kill himself if I didn't tell him where you were.

    Those threats kept me on edge—just like the tension and uncertainty I felt growing up.

    I was so angry at him, but at the same time, I was terrified that this time he really meant it. I feel stupid now, in retrospect, but I was so worried that I booked a flight to Alaska just to make sure he was okay. I thought maybe, if I was there, I could stop him from doing something irreversible. I

Dear Red Straw

realize now how futile that was. It was never my responsibility to save him. But back then, it felt like it was.

Dad, when you found out I was coming, your threats stopped. Suddenly, you seemed happy—like my visit was fixing everything. I took time off work that I didn't have, unpaid, put my life and my own family in Texas on hold, just to be there for you.

I'll never forget getting off that plane, riding down the escalator, feeling stupidly excited that you were finally happy to see me. But the second we made eye contact, I knew.

The smile on your face faded instantly, eyebrows slanting into disappointment, your whole expression tightening with growing anger.

And in that moment, I understood.

You weren't excited about me. You had hoped I was bringing Mom back with me.

That's why, when you saw I was alone, you weren't just let down—you were furious. You saw me as a tool, a pawn to help you win her back. And when you realized I wasn't that, I didn't matter anymore.

I wanted to turn around and get right back on that plane. I even tried to change my ticket a few days later, but I couldn't afford the cost. I was trapped there for a week. Trapped with you.

Every day was the same. You'd start drinking the second you got off work, and by nightfall, you were too far gone to move. You'd pass out on the couch, and I'd sleep on the floor. Some nights, I'd find you sprawled across the kitchen tiles, seemingly unconscious, your body limp and unmovable.

I listened to you rant—nonstop—about how unfair life was to you, how Mom had abandoned you, how none of it was your fault.

I became so depressed that, for the first time in my life, I understood what it felt like to want to die.

I remember thinking: If this is my life forever, I don't want it.

Dear Red Straw

The day I got to leave, I felt nothing but relief. That trip was a brutal, inescapable reminder of how far gone my relationship with both of you had become.

I wish I could say I stopped hoping after that. That I stopped believing things could change. But hope is a stubborn thing. And for too long, it kept me coming back, trying to fix something that was never mine to fix.

CHAPTER 3

SWORN TO SECRECY

Secrets. They do more than just hide the truth—they rot it. Like a spoiled banana—bright, smooth, inviting on the outside—but peel back the layers, and you find bruises, soft spots, and damage you didn't expect.

They're silent. Shameful. Passed down from one generation to the next—like family heirlooms. The rules no one says out loud: "We don't talk about that."

Silence doesn't ease the pain. It just adds to it. The person drinking hides the truth to keep from facing it, and because hiding has simply become part of the habit.

The people around them—the ones hurt the most—hide it too, out of fear, shame, or the need to protect the family from looking bad. The truth gets buried under guilt, denial, and the pressure to pretend everything's fine.

But that pressure doesn't just sit on the person keeping the secret—it spreads to everyone living inside the lie. And no matter how deep you try to bury the truth, it always finds its way back to the surface.

Hiding the drinking isn't all that different from hiding anything else. Maybe you stole something and convinced yourself it wasn't a big deal—so you never admitted it, even when you had the chance to make it right.

Maybe you got emotionally close to someone outside your relationship and told yourself it didn't really count because it wasn't physical.

We all find ways to make things seem smaller, softer, and easier to ignore when we're not ready to see the truth.

You've told yourself your drinking is under control, thinking that as long as no one is bothered by it, no one's getting hurt.

You hide it from yourself, but it's not hidden. It's coming out—it already has.

The damage isn't just about what's been covered up—it's what it does to the people around you. The betrayal. The broken trust. The painful moment when someone who loves you realizes you haven't been honest with them.

I can't pretend I've always been honest either. I've hidden things, looked away, convinced myself of what I wanted to believe.

As an adult, I'd pick my mom up for errands and family gatherings. I'd recognize the smell right away—sour, sweet, and sharp, like fruit rotting in the sun.

She'd try to act like everything was fine, saying she hadn't had anything to drink. But I knew better.

Dear Red Straw

Sometimes I'd speak up and tell her I could smell it. She'd deny it over and over, making me feel like I was the one who was wrong.

Other times, I stayed quiet. I told myself she wasn't that drunk. I didn't want the fight. I didn't want to be upset.

And it wasn't just the alcohol.

Painkillers. She'd always say she was following the directions on the bottle, never taking more than her prescription said she could.

But the signs were there—the slurred words, how tired she always looked, the glassy eyes. The way she'd stumble when she walked.

And it always felt impossible to tell which one she was on—the pills, the alcohol, or both.

She'd say she was sober, just tired. Or she'd say the medications were too strong.

Other times, she'd say she wasn't taking any medications at all—that it was just one drink.

She'd talk about needing a refill on her pills for pain and anxiety—saying she was almost out, that she couldn't get by without them

Then be turned away at the pharmacy because she was trying to fill them too soon.

I stood beside her in those lines, watching her argue with the pharmacists, trying to convince them they had made a mistake—only to lose the battle every time.

We'd walk out, her frustrated, blaming them. Saying it was all their fault. But I knew better.

There was one day I'll never forget.

She had run out of pills early. The pharmacy told her she had to wait a week to refill them, and when that week was up, she was already falling apart.

We stood at the front of the line. Her hands trembling. Eyes wide. Restless, and uneasy—like she was trying to crawl out of her own skin. I could feel the tension coming off her—it was so strong I thought if I leaned against it, it would hold me up.

From the corner of my eye, I saw an elderly woman shuffle toward the counter and cut in front of us, even though we were next.

She moved with that same jittery, wound-up energy my mom had. I tensed up. I already knew—there was no way my mom was letting that slide.

"Excuse me, ma'am, you just cut in front of us and we're next," my mom snapped, her voice filled with frustration.

"I was next!" the woman proclaimed, turning toward my mom, then back to the pharmacist in a rush, pretending we weren't even there.

"Excuse me, ma'am, I'm on disability and I was next!" my mom yelled.

"I'm on disability too—and I was next!"

Not wanting to get involved, but knowing I had to, I stepped in. "Ma'am, it's fine. Just go ahead—we'll go after you."

Dear Red Straw

We stood there in silence, my mom not saying another word. I could feel the heat coming off her—like heat from summer pavement. Hands were still shaking. Eyes locked on the counter, trying to hold herself together by force. Not from embarrassment—this wasn't about feeling shame. It was pressure. Rage. Desperation.

Like something inside her was clawing to get out and had nowhere to go.

I didn't fully understand the "disability" remark until later. In her mind, being on disability justified everything—why she needed the pills, why the drinking wasn't a problem, why none of this was her fault.

The pills and the alcohol helped numb the pain—but that reason became the excuse. And somewhere along the way, numbing the pain turned into abusing the very things that were supposed to help.

If the pain was real—and it was—then maybe, to her, the rest of it could be forgiven. Maybe if she could convince herself of that, she wouldn't have to face what was really going on.

But I saw it. I was standing right there beside her. And I said nothing.

The longer the lie stays alive, the more it costs—trust, closeness, connection. It doesn't ease the pain. It multiplies it.

But secrets don't stay hidden forever. And when it comes to alcoholism, keeping it a secret isn't protecting anyone. It's just allowing the cycle to continue.

Jeremy Allen Damours

It's sort of tragic—how much effort my parents put into hiding their drinking. They thought they were being clever, like they had us kids completely fooled.

And for a long time, they did.

They were masters at making it look normal—hiding it in plain sight by turning it into routine. We didn't know any better.

And outside the house, they managed it just enough to stay unnoticed.

But the truth has a way of telling on itself. As they got older, the drinking started to show. It wore down their bodies. They slipped up more often. The cracks in their carefully held image got bigger, and it became clear—no matter how hard they tried, people were starting to see through it.

And in a small town like ours, hiding only worked for so long.

When I was growing up, everyone in our town seemed to know each other—and each other's business. That made it hard to keep anything private, especially when it came to drinking. My dad didn't want people to know how often he was buying alcohol, so he made sure to never go to the same place too often—to make it less obvious.

One day, he'd stop at the Oaken Keg to buy a handle of whiskey. A day or two later, he'd swing by the Walmart liquor store. Then Safeway a day or two after that.

Dear Red Straw

He made sure not to shop at the same place too often in a row. He spaced it out just enough so no cashier would recognize him as the guy buying whiskey every other day.

To them, he probably looked like a casual drinker—just picking something up for the weekend or a special occasion.

But in reality, he was keeping the house stocked with alcohol all the time.

And it didn't matter if the weather was bad or the drive was out of the way—if it was time to buy, he went.

Anything to keep the drinking going without drawing attention.

My dad's drink of choice was Canadian Mist or Jack Daniel's, always mixed with 7 Up.

He had a routine for how he made his drinks—three parts whiskey, one part soda, always sipped through a skinny red straw.

If he couldn't find his straw—or worse, if someone had left it in the sink, sitting in old food or floating in dirty dish water—he'd explode.

"God DAMN it, Kathy!" he'd yell at my mom, sometimes slamming his fists on the counter, furious that his straw was missing or filthy.

It was never his fault.

As long as the straw was clean and right where he left it, he was fine. But if not, his mood went bad fast.

My mom preferred rum and Coke.

Jeremy Allen Damours

She mixed her drinks the same way my dad did—mostly alcohol, just a splash of soda to make it go down easier.

But unlike him, she didn't need a straw. No rituals, no red straw set aside like it was sacred. Just the drink.

The smell of their drinks lingers in my memory. Sharp, sour, stinging. The kind of scent that fills your nose and makes your eyes water before it hits your throat. It hung around their cups like paint thinner—bitter fumes, strong and hard to ignore.

But like the smell of their drinks, the truth clung to everything—stronger with time.

Years after I moved out, the accidents started. Embarrassing moments they could no longer cover up. They were getting too worn down to keep hiding it.

They were renting a small apartment near the river. Their landlord lived right upstairs. My dad liked to step outside late at night and stare at the water—especially in the summer, when the midnight sun painted the sky in soft pastels. My mom would follow him. To keep him company. To keep him from falling into the river, drunk.

One night, as they were heading back inside, he tripped and fell just feet from their door—outside their landlord's laundry room window, in full view. Too drunk to get up.

Panicked, my mom tried to pull him up, but he was dead weight. She couldn't lift him, and he was too drunk to help. He just lay there, slurring, yelling at her

Dear Red Straw

to drag him inside before anyone saw. The more she struggled, the louder he got—until their landlord came to the window.

She finally managed to get him through the door, but she knew they'd been caught. And this wasn't the first time. Next time, they might not just get caught—they might get kicked out.

They thought they were keeping it together. But little by little, the truth was showing. In their faces. In their bodies. In the way they were falling apart.

Jeremy Allen Damours

Doctor's appointments with my dad weren't easy. As he got older and his health started slipping, the truth got harder to ignore. I didn't always go with him, but that day, I was just around—and somehow ended up in the passenger seat.

We sat in the exam room, quiet. No windows, no sunlight—just white walls and that sterile feeling I've always hated. My dad, filling out the form they gave him, scribbling away, and me, staring at the small silver bin on the counter next to the cotton balls and soap.

I've never liked exam rooms. They feel too clean—cold, bright, distant.

Like a place built to hold bad news.

No warmth, no comfort. Just hard floors and that tense kind of silence that makes you more aware of your own mortality.

These are the rooms where private things are said out loud, where the body is exposed, and where truth tends to come in quiet, heavy blows.

Even when you're healthy, you don't want to be here.

And when you're not—well, these rooms have a way of making it feel worse.

The doctor walked in without much expression, clipboard in hand, already mid-sentence. She barely looked up—just ran through her questions like she was checking boxes, not speaking to a person.

Dear Red Straw

"Do you drink or smoke?"

He didn't hesitate. Just looked at her and said, "No."

And just like that, she moved on—no follow-up, no second glance, as if his answer was enough.

He continued answering her questions like nothing was wrong.

Left out the drinking, the skipped meds, the days he'd fall into things.

Sitting there, listening to him pretend everything was fine, made me feel invisible. Like the truth didn't matter.

I kept quiet, but inside, I was angry—he kept lying, like the problem wasn't right there between us.

I wanted to scream. I wanted to interrupt and say, actually, he drinks every single day. A lot. But I didn't.

I just sat there, silent, holding in my anger. It was building up inside me, but I didn't feel like I had permission to let it out.

Saying something would have felt like betraying my dad, and I knew he'd be furious with me for telling the truth.

And I didn't want to start a fight.

It's the corner you get backed into when you love an alcoholic.

You learn to think through every word, decide which truths are worth the trouble, and let the rest go—

because deep down, you know saying something won't lead to change.

It just brings more stress, more denial, and more reasons for them to drink.

I loved my dad. I didn't want to make things harder for him.

But the doctor didn't know.

If she had, maybe she could've helped him stop drinking—helped him see what the alcohol was doing to his body.

But I already knew how that would go. He wasn't going to accept help.

Maybe that's why I stayed quiet. I already knew it wouldn't change a thing.

Dear Red Straw

My dad wasn't ashamed of his addiction. He drank with an arrogance—like it gave him power. At home, he never hid it. He didn't owe anyone an explanation. Nothing to regret.

But away from home, he cared deeply about his image. That's when the act changed. No one would've known how deep the problem really went.

He was unapologetically an alcoholic—and proud of it.

My mom was different. She was apologetically an alcoholic.

She drank in front of us growing up, but not like my dad. There was hesitation in it—like she didn't want to be seen, but couldn't stop herself either.

As we got older and moved out, things changed. She started hiding it more—watching her words on the phone, keeping it tucked away during visits. The shame grew stronger once we weren't kids anymore.

Still, she kept drinking. I believe she felt guilty. Maybe even ashamed. But not enough to stop. That takes a certain kind of boldness too—not loud like my dad's, but just as stubborn.

Before he died, when his mind was still clear, he told us to take care of our mother if anything ever happened to him. I said we would—not knowing what I was really agreeing to.

He had always been the one in charge. The one who handled everything. Without him, she would be lost. And the drinking would only get worse.

It wasn't until after he died that I saw just how much he had controlled her.

For years, he stripped her of nearly every freedom.

He never let her get a driver's license, never let her make big financial decisions, never let her vote, or go out with friends.

He told her what to wear.

And if he didn't say it, a look was enough.

He controlled the money, the house, the family—his voice was the final word on everything.

And over time, that wore her down.

When he died, she wasn't just grieving—she was lost.

She had no idea how to be independent, how to function in the world without someone telling her what to do.

She was already drinking—but now, with no one running her or the house, it got worse.

Her days went without routine.

No job. No one telling her what to do.

Just hours to kill—and alcohol to fill them.

Dear Red Straw

She got a monthly check, spent every dollar, then rushed to figure out where the next chunk of money would come from.

Bills didn't get paid.

Food barely made it into the house.

Toilet paper, groceries, laundry detergent—none of it mattered if there was liquor to buy.

That's when she started coming to us.

She had a system.

One day she'd ask me, the next day my brother, then the next.

The reasons didn't change.

Said she needed a co-pay for a doctor's visit. Or a medical bill was about to go to collections.

Sometimes she'd say she was just a little short and needed fifty bucks—always promising to pay it back when her check came in.

At first, we believed her.

But over time, we started talking—and the stories didn't line up.

She told each of us something different. Different reasons. Different excuses.

She couldn't keep her lies in order.

It was obvious the money was going to alcohol.

When we brought it up, she denied it like she believed it herself—and we'd end up doubting ourselves. She'd act hurt, like we were being unfair just for asking, and say she was telling the truth—even when we knew better.

Still, we kept giving her money. She'd somehow pay it back, but right after she did, she'd ask for more. It happened so often, money was always gone—paid back just long enough for her to ask again.

And it got worse.

When we started saying no, she turned to payday loans—and they helped, like we had. But when she was late, they weren't so nice. The nonstop calls. The threats. She was stuck with them too—borrowing just to pay off the last one.

This should've been her wake-up call. But we always rescued her. We felt bad. We bailed her out.

What were we supposed to do? We couldn't let her end up on the street.

But she couldn't live with me again—not after everything.

My dad's words— "take care of your mother"—didn't feel like something I'd agreed to anymore. They felt like a curse.

Dear Red Straw

Looking back, it got harder to ignore what had always been there. My parents' drinking wasn't just background noise—it was the center of everything. Once I saw it clearly, I felt exposed. So I covered for them—but really, I was trying to hide myself.

I didn't like bringing people around. And when I had to, I played along like everything was fine. The looks. The comments. The things no one said, but I could still feel. The hardest part wasn't knowing the truth—it was pretending it wasn't there.

So when a family reunion came up, part of me didn't know what to expect.

My partner and I flew out with our boys. We all ended up at a pizza place in a mall, where—for the first time in decades—grandparents, aunts, uncles, cousins, and siblings were all together.

It wasn't long after the awkward introductions—from being apart for so long—that we started to relax and reconnect.

As the afternoon went on, I kept looking at my parents, watching their faces. For a while, I had stopped thinking about the looks or the stares.

I had stopped pretending everything was fine, because I was caught up in the moment—lost in good company.

I glanced at my dad, then looked away. A moment later, I looked back—and I knew. He was having a hard time being there. He was trying to hold it in.

I knew that look too well—sober, but uncomfortable. He was doing his best just to get through it. And I could feel it in his body, in the way he kept fidgeting, checking his watch like he was counting down the minutes.

In that moment I didn't care. Being around family—something that almost never happened—had my attention somewhere else. I wasn't trying to think about what might go wrong.

I didn't know what was coming later that evening.

After pizza, we all headed to a burger spot for more food, dessert, and to keep the conversation going. We were having a good time—laughing, catching up, enjoying each other. We didn't get much of that growing up.

But I was still watching him. My dad. Fidgeting, checking the time, doing his best to hang on.

And then it happened. He did what I'd been waiting for him to do all night—make an excuse to leave early. Said he and my mom needed to go to bed for their morning flight.

No one questioned it. We hugged them goodbye and stayed a while longer, just holding onto the moment.

Later, we headed back to the hotel, planning to end the night with a family swim. But as we walked toward the pool, we saw them—sitting outside,

Dear Red Straw

drinking. They weren't asleep. They weren't even in their room.

Silence followed as we all took in the scene. Some traded looks—not with blame, but with quiet disappointment.

I felt angry.

Angry that my parents had lied.

Angry that, once again, alcohol came before us.

But more than anything, I felt embarrassed.

Embarrassed in front of my family as they watched it all unfold. Embarrassed that I'd spent years trying to hide a secret they already knew.

I couldn't keep pretending. Not when it was right there—out in the open, for everyone to see.

Jeremy Allen Damours

We don't always know how heavy secrets are—until we've carried them so long, they catch up to us. Usually when we're at our lowest.

And not all of those secrets come from the person drinking.

There's another kind—one that's harder to name, but just as heavy. It's the one the rest of us keep: that we're exhausted, overwhelmed, and silently drowning in the weight of everything they've handed to us. And we never say it out loud.

It's like they hand you a suitcase full of their problems—the lies, the guilt, the messes they leave behind—and expect you to carry it without saying a word.

We don't tell them it's too heavy. We don't ask why we're the ones holding it. We just keep dragging it around, pretending we're fine.

Sometimes we're scared that saying something will make things worse—or push them even deeper into the drinking. And sometimes, staying quiet feels like the only way to keep our own lives from falling apart.

It's no wonder we keep it to ourselves.

Over time, keeping everything in wears us down. We stop trusting ourselves. We stop being honest about how we're really doing. We ignore our stress, bottle up our anger, and pretend like we're fine—just to get through the day. And the longer we do that, the worse it gets.

Dear Red Straw

We tell ourselves we're keeping the peace, but really, we're just making it easier for them to keep doing what they're doing. The stress wears us down—we don't sleep, we gain weight, we stop enjoying the things that used to make us feel alive. We're too drained from holding everything together. And while we're breaking down, they walk away feeling lighter. They've handed us their suitcase and called it love, or family, or our responsibility.

I didn't really understand this until later—when my mom came to stay with my partner and me after my dad died.

By then, she had already been staying with us for a while—and she was doing the same things I'd seen her do my whole life. The same behaviors I thought I'd finally gotten away from. When I left home, I thought I was done with all that. But now she was in my home, and it all came back with her. The drinking. The lies. The way she relied on me like I was the only one who could hold her together.

One morning, we ran into each other in the kitchen. I had been avoiding her. I didn't want to deal with any of it—not the stress, not the tension, not the pretending.

I was in a bad mood, and she could tell. She was always good at picking up on things like that, so she kept pushing, asking what was wrong. I didn't want to talk. I didn't want to get pulled into another one of our exhausting, back-and-forth conversations where I had to pretend everything was fine.

She told me she felt like something was off between us. That I seemed cold. Distant.

But I wasn't trying to be. I was just worn down. Worn down by the apologies that didn't mean much anymore. Worn down by how easily she took things the wrong way—if I left without saying goodbye, if my partner and I went out alone, if I asked her not to feed the dog scraps. Even if I was just reading or playing a game to unwind, she'd take it as me avoiding her.

And every time I tried to set a boundary, it turned into another conversation, another round of "I'm sorry." She always felt better after saying it. But I was the one left dealing with it.

So I snapped.

"I'm tired of the lies," I told her.

I wasn't just talking about the drinking. I was talking about everything. The times she was clearly drunk but swore she wasn't. The times she borrowed money for groceries or bills, but I knew exactly where it was going. The times she made me feel guilty for not giving more of myself—more time, more energy—even when I had nothing left to give.

She didn't argue. She didn't deny it. She just stood there—quiet, like she finally understood.

That moment made me realize something else.

I'd spent so long covering up the things my parents did—the drinking, the lies, the chaos—that hiding my own pain started to feel normal too. I could talk about everyday things. But the deeper stuff—the

Dear Red Straw

fear, the shame, the parts of me that actually needed to be seen—I kept all that to myself.

I could talk about things like work stress, a bad night's sleep, or how long the grocery lines were—things that felt safe to share. But when it came to the real stuff—like how ashamed I felt when my mom would lie to me, how guilty I felt for setting boundaries, or how I sometimes questioned whether I was lovable at all—I stayed quiet. For so long, admitting that something was wrong didn't even feel like an option.

But bottling things up doesn't make them disappear. It just leaves you feeling more alone than ever.

It's easy to think that self-care is something extra—something nice to have when there's time. But when you grow up around addiction, it's not extra. It's survival. Every time you deal with someone who needs to vent, be comforted, or be saved from another mess they created, it takes something out of you. It drains your energy, your patience, and whatever strength you have left.

If you don't stop to rest, you burn out. Not just tired—worn down. And when life gets hard, there's nothing left in you to keep going.

If I've learned anything, it's this: no one else is going to let go of that weight for you. You have to be the one to put it down.

Jeremy Allen Damours

Alcoholics will often cover for other alcoholics. In my family, my mom covered for my dad. She made excuse after excuse. For the drinking, the outbursts, the accidents. Like it was her job to protect him from the truth. She thought she was helping. But she wasn't. It made things worse.

The chaos would start at night and carry into the morning. If my dad had tripped and fallen, she'd excuse it as clumsiness.

When we found steak knives stuck between the couch cushions—left behind after he passed out mid-meal, sharp ends pointing up—she'd insist it was just an accident. We nearly sat on them more than once.

If he had gone on one of his loud, rambling sprees—accusing people at work of trying to get him fired, claiming the family was against him—she'd wave it off.

"He didn't mean it," she'd say. "He wasn't that drunk."

But he was.

He was always that drunk.

And the worst part? He believed every word he said in those moments. He'd make himself believe we were up to something we weren't. He'd get worked up, easily upset, and impossible to talk to. He'd repeat himself over and over. And the moment we saw a chance to leave, we took it—relieved to escape.

Dear Red Straw

My mom was good at reshaping the story. She'd tell us he apologized—and in the same breath, say he didn't remember any of what we said happened. It didn't make sense. Somehow, what happened the night before was now just a misunderstanding. Her version of things never added up. It felt like she was shifting the blame onto us, like we were too sensitive. Like we were the ones who were wrong.

It left me questioning what I'd seen with my own eyes.

Secrets have a way of keeping things looking polished—like nothing's wrong. Like a flower garden in full bloom—bright, quiet, untouched. But when you lean in to water the plants, you spot something small: clusters of tiny eggs clinging to the underside of a leaf. So you check another. And another. Soon, you realize it's everywhere. What looked beautiful from a distance is already breaking down. The damage was there all along—you just hadn't gotten close enough to see it.

Alcoholism is the same. From a distance, things look fine. Outsiders don't see the damage—because they're kept at arm's length. And the alcoholics? They get really good at hiding the truth.

But the people closest to them? We know the truth. We feel the impact. And over time, we start putting together what's really going on.

And then we get pulled into the same cycle—trying to help, getting worn down, stepping away, only to come back and try again.

Jeremy Allen Damours

It's a lonely place to live. A secret you want to share but can't. A truth you're desperate to speak—but don't.

And for so many years, I didn't.

Dear Red Straw

For years, I thought silence was a form of protection. That hiding my parents' drinking, covering for their mistakes, and explaining away their behavior was the only way to keep the peace. But silence doesn't protect anyone. It just delays the damage.

I used to think that breaking the silence meant turning my back on them. That talking about their alcoholism was letting them down. But I see it differently now. It's not about shaming or punishing them. It's about healing.

Secrecy gives addiction room to grow. It lets it hide in the dark, untouched and unquestioned. And the more we protect the lie, the more we help the cycle keep going. But when we speak the truth—when we stop pretending—we make space for something different.

I carried the burden of secrecy for a long time. I let it shape how I moved through the world, how much of myself I showed, how much truth I allowed in. But when I stopped holding onto their secrets, I realized I didn't have to keep living that way.

And neither do you.

Addiction isolates people. But healing doesn't. Healing happens when we stop hiding. When we say, "This is what happened." "This is what I survived." "This is how I'm moving forward."

Keeping secrets kept me small. It made me doubt what I knew to be true. It made it hard to trust other people—and myself. But breaking the silence gave me back my power.

If you're still carrying someone else's secrets, know this: You can put them down. You can tell the truth. You can choose a different path.

Because the only way to stop the cycle is to refuse to be a part of it any longer.

Dear Red Straw

Dear Mom,

I felt torn when you told me Grandpa Ron was dying and how badly you wanted me to go with you to see him. I remember thinking it was strange that Dad wasn't going with you— he never let you out of his sight, never let you travel alone. I still wonder if that was some kind of divine intervention because I think the trip would have been so much worse if he had. In a way, I was relieved he stayed behind.

I felt just as conflicted about meeting you in Phoenix, our planes converging into one path— yours from Alaska, mine from Texas. I knew how much you wanted to see your dad before he passed. I did too. But I also knew why you asked me to go, and even though I wanted to, I never called you out on it. You didn't just need company. You needed someone to drive you around, to handle the logistics, to do the things Dad always did because, for the first time, he wasn't there to control the situation. You needed a stand-in. And that made me angry.

Jeremy Allen Damours

Because once again, it felt like you were manipulating me into doing something for you. Something you needed but couldn't do on your own. Yeah, I'm sure you wanted me there. But wanting me there wasn't your first motivation. I know that might sound selfish given the circumstances—Grandpa was dying, after all—but that doesn't make it any less true.

There were plenty of times growing up when you gave me selfless love. But the older I got, the further you seemed to slip into a childlike version of yourself, getting deeper into your alcoholism, manipulating the people who loved you most—me, Josh, Chris, Aunt Terry. The deeper you got, the further away you became. Distant. Lost. When you did emerge, it wasn't for us. It was for alcohol. Can you see now why it felt less like you wanted me there and more like you needed me there?

That day was long. We both traveled for hours—you had your flight from the top of the world, I had my layovers. When I finally saw you in the airport that night, you looked hollowed out. Exhausted. Fading.

Dear Red Straw

Like there wasn't much fight left in you. And the first thing you did when we got to the hotel at 1 a.m.? You somehow found alcohol. To this day, I don't even know how—you made sure we didn't stop anywhere, nothing was open. But there it was, like it had been waiting for you. You needed your hit so the withdrawals wouldn't come for you in the night.

The next few days were some of the hardest I've ever experienced. Maybe they were for you too, though I don't know if you'd admit it. Every morning, you'd wake up and start drinking. Then we'd go see Grandpa in the nursing home. It never failed—after a couple of hours, you'd lean over to me, whisper that we had to leave, and then tell Grandpa and Aunt Terry some excuse about needing to take care of things. Sometimes we came back later. Other times we didn't.

You couldn't tell them the truth. And Grandpa was too far gone to understand.

It was humiliating to be part of that lie, pretending we had somewhere important to be when all you really needed was to get back to the hotel to drink. I wanted so badly to tell the truth. To say it out loud. To expose you in some desperate hope that the shame of it would make you stop. But I kept quiet. I always kept quiet.

I sat in that hotel room with you, watching you top off your rum with Coke over and over, feeling nothing but rage and grief. Alcohol had been stealing you from me for years, but I had never seen it so clearly as I did on that trip.

That trip was dark.

A trip I hope I never have to take again.

Chapter 4

Bound By Shame and Guilt

What if the people you looked to for love and security were the same ones who made you feel unlovable?

That was my dad.

Back when we lived in Arizona, I don't remember much about my dad. He was gone most days, working at a trucking company—first washing trucks, then eventually driving them. When he got home after work, he'd grab a beer, sit down, and watch television. He mostly kept to himself, and there wasn't much interaction between him and us—not a lot of talking, not a lot of hugs.

But I remember one afternoon when I was five years old. He was in a good mood and asked me to sit on his lap to play. He smiled and hugged me. It should've felt warm and safe—but instead, it felt strange, because he wasn't usually interested in me.

I didn't know what to do with his attention. I sat stiff on his lap while he bounced me on his knee, flopped my arms around, and laughed like we were having fun. But it felt awkward. I didn't know how to go along with it. And maybe that's what made it uncomfortable—because it did feel real, like he actually wanted to connect, and I wasn't used to that. I felt uneasy. Suspicious. Like something about him couldn't be trusted.

My Uncle Michael didn't make me feel that way.

He was different. When he'd visit on weekends, he paid attention to me and my brothers. He'd pull us into his lap, talk with us, play with us—and I never felt that same weirdness. Being around him felt natural in a way it never did with my father.

He gave us a taste of what it could feel like to be seen and wanted by the man who was supposed to be that for us.

At the time, I didn't think much of leaving Uncle Michael behind when we moved. It wasn't until years later that I realized how much it had meant to feel cared about like that.

I was seven when we left Arizona and made our way to Alaska. My dad was drinking more, and whatever little connection we had just stayed like that. It never became anything more.

As a kid, it's hard to make sense of what's happening. You start looking for answers, even though you don't really know what you're looking for. And it messes with you—because you still trust your dad, even while you're feeling both love and pain. You soak up his moods and copy what he does, not knowing yet that it's not a pattern you're supposed to follow.

By the time I was twelve came another move—back to Arizona. My mom's idea, probably chasing a

Dear Red Straw

closeness she hadn't felt with her sister in years. But we weren't going back to the area where Uncle Michael had lived. That connection was already gone. We hadn't heard from him—or that side of the family—in a long time.

My dad was out of work for most of that time in Arizona while my mom worked at the town's title company. No one would even give him an interview, and nothing he found paid enough. The town we moved to was small, mostly made up of Mormon families. We were outsiders, and they made it clear pretty quickly that we weren't welcome. The staredowns at the grocery store. The way people refused to make eye contact or shake hands when we met them. The gossip that made its way back to us—about how so-and-so didn't like us because we weren't one of them. My parents had no interest in religion, and no intention of trying to fit in. We struggled to make ends meet.

But not having money didn't stop them from scraping together what they could to keep the cabinets stocked with alcohol.

Without work to distract him, the tension in the house thickened. He was home all the time, and we felt the full weight of his silence—and his anger. The little things kids do—leaving messes around the house, running in and out to play and tracking in dirt, using tools in the backyard and forgetting to put them away—set him off. But nothing got to him more than a messy kitchen.

He'd clean the kitchen by 11 a.m. and proclaim, "Kitchen's closed!" As if we didn't need to eat again that day.

By afternoon, he'd always say the same thing: "Save your appetite for dinner!" If we didn't want to go hungry, breakfast had to keep us full the rest of the day.

On days when he'd leave the house for a job interview or an errand, we'd sneak into the kitchen—cleaning up every crumb and making sure the dishes were washed and put away, so he wouldn't know we'd been there.

I didn't realize how much I'd internalized it until years later—when I had kids of my own.

One day, I found myself getting irritated at the mess my boys were making in the kitchen. Without even thinking, I firmly announced, "Kitchen's closed!"

The words had barely left my mouth before it hit me.

I had a flashback to the times my dad would make that same announcement—the uncertainty I felt, the fear of getting caught eating when I was hungry.

I felt awful.

I whispered, "Oh my God, you're turning into your father."

And that wasn't the first time I had felt the weight of his words living in me.

There was that moment—years earlier—that still stuck with me. My dad, drunk and cold, looking at us and saying, "I will always love your mother more than I love you."

I was still a kid. I didn't know how to make sense of that. I just believed it. I figured I had done

Dear Red Straw

something wrong. That I wasn't enough. That maybe he wished I wasn't there at all.

So later, when I heard those same kinds of things coming out of my own mouth, I wasn't just repeating his words. I was passing on the same shame I'd carried around for years. The guilt of feeling like a bother. Of taking up space. Of doing something wrong just by needing something as simple as food.

That's the thing about shame and guilt—they aren't always obvious. Sometimes they just simmer in the background, quietly shaping how we feel about ourselves, how we act, and how we treat people. And letting go of them isn't just about understanding the past. It's about choosing, every day, not to let them run your life.

I found myself as a child looking for the reasons—trying to figure out why my dad felt the way he did about me. Was it because I was a premature twin who needed extra care, stealing all of my mom's attention? Were my brothers and I just obstacles, keeping him from the life he wanted? Did he just hate being a father?

I started to wonder if I was part of the reason he drank. If I had pushed him further into it.

That's when the shame and guilt really started to shape how I saw myself.

Jeremy Allen Damours

By the time I was in my early twenties, I still felt like I wasn't good enough. Like I didn't belong anywhere. Like I wasn't worthy of love or acceptance. I felt misunderstood—by others, and even myself.

Maybe that's part of why I got married young. I was still trying to find where I fit, trying to create something safe that made me feel whole.

We were young and just starting to build a life together when we had Nathaniel.

And then we lost him to a rare genetic disease when he was only a year old.

After he died, my wife and I started going to church. We were looking for meaning—something to help us make sense of our loss. We needed a reason to keep going, and we thought maybe God could give us one.

Not long after we started attending, the pastor's wife invited us to their Home Friendship Group—a small weekly get-together meant to help people connect with each other, and with God.

Home Friendship Group was like a midweek church service—but instead of meeting at the church, we met at someone's house. We'd eat snacks, talk, sing songs, and go over a lesson. While the same couple hosted and led the group each week, the rest of us took turns bringing food.

One night, the couple leading the group brought up the idea of taking turns meeting at each other's

Dear Red Straw

homes. At the time, my wife and I were staying with my parents while we tried to save money and get back on our feet. But the moment I heard the idea, I panicked—there was no way I could let the group meet at our place with my parents drinking in the next room.

I immediately started scrambling for an excuse—anything that would let me say no without embarrassing myself or my parents. I couldn't risk the group seeing my dad drunk, hearing one of his out-of-place comments, or getting caught in one of his outbursts.

It's strange that I was worried about my parents being embarrassed, too. After everything they'd put me through, I had every reason to only care about looking out for myself. But I didn't want them doing something they'd be ashamed of once they sobered up. I still loved them, even when they made it hard—and part of me still wanted to protect them, too.

That's what made it so messy. I wasn't just worried about what might happen right then—I was thinking about what would come after. What would my Home Friendship Group leaders think? What would my pastor say if he found out I had brought members of his congregation into a home where my dad was drinking and yelling? What if word spread through the church?

I felt bad that I couldn't help out like everyone else. I wanted to take a turn, but there was no way I could let people come over and see my parents drinking.

I could tell the truth or make something up.

But I was too ashamed to tell the truth.

So I lied.

I told them my dad wasn't into church stuff and wouldn't be okay with us having the group over.

And then, I felt bad about that too.

It wasn't a complete lie—my dad wasn't a Christian. But he didn't have a problem with it either. He didn't care about religion. I never really knew what he believed.

What if letting my Home Friendship Group meet at our place had made him curious enough to look at his own life?

What if seeing people trying to live better and take care of themselves had made him want to do the same?

What if that night could've been the push he needed to stop drinking and turn things around?

But deep down, I knew the truth.

My dad was never going to give up drinking—not for anyone or anything.

Still, I was torn.

I was embarrassed about my home life.

I felt bad for lying.

And I felt just as bad for not being honest about what was really going on.

No matter what I did, I always felt like it was up to me to keep things from getting out of control. It wasn't just about lying—it was about constantly trying to manage the chaos around me.

Dear Red Straw

I was doing everything I could think of to keep us together. Church every Sunday. Staying committed to Home Friendship Group. Trying to be the man I promised I'd be. But our marriage was quietly falling apart behind the scenes.

Having two more boys after Nathaniel died felt like a second chance, and I threw myself into being everything I thought I should be—a steady husband, a present father, a man of faith. But we were both still grieving. Still changing. Trying to become people for each other that we weren't within ourselves—just to keep the marriage alive.

In the end, we had to stop pretending and face the mirror.

I was the one still trying to make church life work. I believed in it. I was living it. She believed too, in her own way—but her heart wasn't in it. Not like mine was. I finally had to face the fact that I was asking her to live a life she didn't want. We might've seemed like we were on the same page in the beginning. But looking back, I think her heart had always been in a different place.

Church didn't feel like home anymore, either. Not because I stopped believing in God—but because I couldn't keep going to the place where I had to hide the part of myself the church didn't see as okay. I was tired of pretending. Tired of keeping quiet. Tired of having to act like someone I wasn't just to be accepted.

Jeremy Allen Damours

And just like that, I was raising two boys by myself.

That's when I met Michael—the man who stayed.

The marriage was over by then. It had been about two years since the divorce—two years of grieving and learning how to be a full-time parent. I had moved to Texas with the boys, hoping for a fresh start, with no real idea what life was going to look like next.

It wasn't easy. I was alone, broke, and doing my best to keep up—raising two kids, working as a nurse, and trying to hold everything together. It was exhausting. I felt isolated, like nobody really understood what I was going through. But I also knew I wasn't the only one. Other parents had done this before—raised kids on their own, made it work. If they could do it, so could I.

I was also trying to date again. I had a couple relationships that felt like they were going somewhere, but they didn't last. One ended because he cheated. The other ended when he told me he wasn't ready to be around kids all the time. It wasn't that my boys were hard to deal with—he just wasn't ready for that kind of life. We were both in our mid-twenties, and I could understand where he was coming from. But that didn't make it hurt any less. After a while, it started to feel like no one was ever going to stay.

But Michael was different—calm, kind, and straightforward. The others were just boys. Some were selfish. Some didn't want anything serious. Some only wanted sex. But Michael didn't run when he saw I had

Dear Red Straw

kids. He didn't make excuses or disappear for days. He was only twenty-three, but he called when he said he would. He showed up when we made plans. He asked questions and actually listened to the answers. None of the others did that.

The more time I spent with Michael, the more I realized how much I wanted to keep him close. He felt like something good I wasn't used to having—and I didn't want to lose it.

There was something else, too—Michael was Black, which didn't feel out of the ordinary to me. I'd always dated outside my race. But being with Michael made me look at things I'd never questioned growing up. Not because of anything about Michael—but because of my family. Sometimes my dad would say things that were racist, and we'd always chalk it up to him being drunk or trying to be funny. It was either laughed off or ignored. I learned to stay quiet, pretend it didn't happen, and avoid a fight—no matter how wrong it felt. I didn't realize how much that had affected me until I saw how badly I handled that night with Michael and my dad.

My parents had just moved to Texas to be closer to me and the kids. At least, that's what it seemed like. I wasn't all that sure. They'd left Alaska before and gone back, so I had a feeling this move might not last either.

We ended up sharing a three-bedroom apartment—me, the boys, and my parents—splitting rent and giving them more time with the kids.

Jeremy Allen Damours

As things settled in, Michael started coming over. Sometimes he stayed the night; other times I stayed at his place while the boys stayed with my parents. I knew their drinking wasn't okay—especially around the boys—but I hadn't been away from it long enough to see how deep it still had its hooks in me. I thought I'd unlearned all that programming. But the second we moved in together, it came right back.

It didn't cross my mind that what felt normal to me might hit Michael like a punch to the gut.

That night, Michael came over after work. It was his turn to stay at my place.

By the time he got there, my dad was already drunk. When he drank, he rambled—loud, unfiltered, whatever came to mind. And sometimes that included racist stuff. Not often. And when it did, it was usually quiet, shrugged off, treated like it wasn't a big deal. So I treated it that way too.

Until that night.

Michael and I were in my room talking when we heard my dad's voice rising in the kitchen. He was ranting about something at work—some coworker he said disrespected him. As he kept talking, his voice got harsher, angrier.

Then, it happened.

He called his coworker the N-word while talking to my mom.

Michael and I locked eyes.

Dear Red Straw

He didn't say anything, but I could see it in his face. Hurt. Angry. Trying not to react.

Panic gripped me.

I scrambled for explanations, desperate for damage control.

"He's not a racist, I swear."

"It has nothing to do with you."

"He just says things when he's drunk—he doesn't mean it. He won't even remember it in the morning, I promise."

Michael wasn't moved by any of it.

The damage was done.

And in that moment, I felt the weight of my father's shame like it was mine.

A jolt of panic tore through me—like lightning, from my chest down to my feet. I could feel it in every inch of my body.

Even though I knew it wasn't me who said it, I still felt responsible.

I knew it was his word, his mess. But I felt the shame too—just for being there. Just for being part of it.

That feeling got worse the second Michael stood up. He didn't raise his voice. Didn't explain. Just said he was going home—that he didn't feel comfortable staying.

I grabbed my keys and followed him toward the door. But when my parents asked where we were going—expecting Michael to stay—I froze. I couldn't bring myself to tell them the truth.

And then the guilt doubled.

I couldn't pretend my dad's words didn't matter anymore. I tried telling myself he was just drunk. That he wouldn't even remember. But I would. And so would Michael.

And the fact that my first instinct had been to protect my father instead of standing up for the person I was falling in love with—that was something I wouldn't forget.

I felt guilty for leaving my boys behind, too. My parents insisted they wanted to watch them—but how could I leave them in the care of two drunk adults?

I didn't even think about the danger. I knew they were drinking, and I still walked out the door.

Dear Red Straw

I was more careful as a child than I was that night.

No one told me to be the responsible one—I just knew it was up to me. Like if I didn't do it, no one else was going to.

I was still a kid, doing whatever I could to make sure we didn't end up dead. I locked the doors at night, checked the stove, and cleared anything that could catch fire near the furnace. I crept through the house like it was my job to keep us alive—because no one else would. While my parents were too drunk to move, I was the one making sure the night didn't end in disaster.

I know I was just a kid—but at the time, it felt like my fault if something happened. Like if I missed something, it meant I hadn't done enough to keep my family safe.

Sometimes someone would leave a pile of clothes too close to the furnace, and that scared the hell out of me. My dad especially—when he was out, he didn't just sleep. He'd argue if you tried to wake him. I don't think even yelling fire would've made him budge.

That fear started young. I was scared of two things: the house catching fire, and someone breaking in and killing us. I'm sure it had something to do with where we lived—way out in the woods, up in the hills outside our small Alaskan town. No streetlights. No neighbors close enough to hear you scream.

Just long, frozen winters and a silence so deep it felt like the woods were listening.

And when the seasons flipped, things didn't feel any safer. In summer, that pale, stretched-out light never fully disappeared—just hovered late into the night, dim and strange, like the sky didn't know what time it was. That kind of light made everything feel exposed. Like something was watching. Waiting.

Then one winter, the thing I feared actually happened.

I was in seventh grade, just back from Christmas break, when my teacher told the class that one of my classmates—Ricky—had lost his home on Christmas Eve. His mom didn't make it out.

I later found out it was a cheap extension cord, and the socket couldn't handle it. It started a fire that spread fast. They had plugged the cord into the heating panel of their car, ran it through a basement window, and into the living room. In Alaska, that kind of thing wasn't unusual—people plugged in their cars so the engines wouldn't freeze. But most used outdoor outlets. Running one inside was a risk.

Ricky was a tall, goofy kid, well-liked by everyone. But when he came back to school weeks later, he wasn't the same.

That fire haunted me. It scared me in a way I'd never forget. After that, I got even more serious about my nightly safety checks.

And even now, as an adult, I still do them.

Dear Red Straw

I check the locks before bed. I make sure the stove is off. I even check the water heater to make sure nothing's too close to it. I walk through the house one last time, just like I did when I was a kid.

I check like it could happen any night.

Jeremy Allen Damours

One fear kept me up at night. But the feeling that I didn't matter was always there, all the time.

Since I was little, I thought I wasn't good enough. Not just unsure of myself—deep down, I believed I was beneath everyone else.

I felt guilty about things most kids wouldn't think about. On days when I was the only one getting dropped off up the hill—when the school bus had to take all those twists and turns just for me—I felt bad for making the other kids wait longer to get home.

If I got called on in class, I stayed quiet. Not because I didn't know the answer, but because I didn't want to be noticed. I already felt like I was in the way at home. My voice didn't feel like it mattered, probably because it didn't around my dad. I kept away from teachers because I didn't want to bother them. I stayed quiet around classmates because I didn't want to annoy anyone or make things weird. I hated being on teams in gym because I thought I was slowing everyone down.

Even standing in line for lunch, I felt like I was holding everyone else up just by being there—like I didn't have the same right to be there as they did.

It was the same with happiness. Feeling joy. Getting excited about something. Wanting to share it with someone. It felt dangerous. Like if I got too happy, something bad would happen. Or someone would ruin it. So I stopped letting myself go there.

Dear Red Straw

My twin brother Josh felt it too—he wanted to be valued, to be worthy, just like I did.

Josh was obsessed with Michael Jackson as a teenager. He'd turn the volume up loud, but sang just under the music, like he didn't want anyone to hear.

He didn't just want to sing—he wanted to be a singer. He even made his own T-shirt with big block letters: DCCT. Dreams Can Come True. He wore it everywhere—at school, around the house—like if he believed in it enough, it would come true.

He wanted to sing so badly, he talked my parents into getting him a music tutor. Once a week, my dad would drive him to his lessons and wait outside in the car, flipping through the newspaper or scribbling on his work orders.

Josh wasn't a bad singer, but his voice never sounded right. His pitch was always a little off, or his tone too shaky—like he was trying to shove the wrong key into a lock. But I knew how much it meant to him. He sang like he had something to prove, like he was trying to show he belonged on stage.

And deep down, I knew he didn't. No matter how many lessons he took, or how hard he practiced, he just didn't have it. And I hated thinking that. Because he never stopped believing. Not in his dream. Not in himself.

That's what made it so hard to watch.

One of his elementary school music teachers once told him he had the kind of voice that could sing opera. He didn't want to sing opera, but hearing that gave him more confidence. Maybe that was all he needed to believe that if he worked hard enough, he could make it. And part of me hoped he could too.

Not long after he started lessons, his vocal coach had him enter a talent show at the library. He hadn't been working on his voice for long, and it still sounded pushed—like he was trying to sing in a way his voice wasn't able to. I don't know if she really believed he was ready, or if she just didn't want to hurt his feelings. Maybe she was just trying to be nice. Or maybe she didn't see how much it would crush him if it didn't go well.

A few nights before the show, he was in his room singing *Remember the Time* and *Man in the Mirror* on repeat. Each time a little louder. Working up the nerve. Starting to really think he could do it.

He really thought they'd see him this time.

And once he believed he could do it, he called Mom and Dad downstairs to sing.

But this wasn't just practice anymore. In his head, he was on stage—already Michael. Feeling every lyric. Adrenaline rushing. The lights. The screams. The dream unfolding right there in his bedroom. And in that moment, all he wanted was to show them—the two people who were supposed to be his biggest fans, to have them believe in him too.

But it was too late. My mom's eyes were already glazed over. Fogged. Distant. She looked at Josh, but he was long gone—already Michael in his mind.

Dear Red Straw

My dad's were the same—glassy, blank. When he drank, it didn't dull him—it made everything meaner.

It wasn't just in what he said—it was how he looked. How he moved. He didn't have to say a word. One stare could slice through the room and make you feel two inches tall.

The way they looked at him made me leave before he even started singing. I knew what kind of punishment was coming.

I hadn't even made it upstairs yet when *Man in the Mirror* started vibrating through the walls. My heart sank.

As Josh sang his heart out, I sat on the couch, waiting—knowing my dad was already boiling under the surface, and Josh's voice was all it would take to make him snap.

All he wanted was for them to listen. To see him. To like his voice. To say they were proud. To find worth in their eyes.

But that chance never came. When the music stopped, I heard the faint voices, followed by the creek of the bedroom door. They stumbled up the stairs, drinks in hand, the ice in their glasses clinking against the silence.

Then came my dad's voice like a sudden slap: "He sounds like a dog." A few cuss words. A sigh, like he was glad it was over.

My mom, trying to soften the blow in a hushed voice. "Danny, he's doing something he loves. We need to support him."

But it was too late.

When I went back downstairs, Josh's face said it all. He looked crushed. Defeated. The light in his eyes, gone.

He never sang again.

Dear Red Straw

Growing up in the mess my parents' drinking left behind made me hold onto a lot of guilt and shame—especially from the things my dad said. It sank in deep. So deep that by the time I was grown, it felt like I'd been tied to a heavy rock and dropped into the ocean. I knew there'd come a point when I'd have to let go of that burden just to make it to the surface so I could breathe.

And I would make it to the surface. But not without scars.

We're all carrying things. Some of it we can see. Some of it we can't. But just because we've been hurt doesn't mean we have to keep carrying it. Showing the scars doesn't mean letting them take over. It just means we're ready to face where they came from—and start finding a way to take the next step.

After my son died when I was nineteen, I started looking for something to help me get through the pain of losing him. I wanted something safe—something that didn't feel like it was going to fall apart at any second.

And once I thought I'd found it, I wanted to share it.

By the time I was twenty-two, I was preaching. I'd had what some people call a Holy Ghost experience, and I believed I'd found my purpose.

I probably should've ended up just like them. An alcoholic. But I wasn't. Their drinking turned me off so much that I wanted nothing to do with it.

It wasn't just about staying away from alcohol. I felt like I'd been lifted out of something that nearly swallowed me—and I wanted the same for them. I wanted to save them from it, the way I believed I'd been saved.

Back then, I saw their drinking as a sickness—something I thought I could fix with faith. I didn't just see it as a bad habit. I thought it was a spiritual battle. I really believed it could send them to hell.

I don't believe that anymore.

I don't see alcoholism as a heaven-or-hell thing. It's personal. It's something people struggle with for all kinds of reasons—emotional, physical, even generational. And if someone believes in God, maybe it gets in the way of that connection. But that's between them and their god. Not me.

I kept asking my parents to come to church, hoping it might help them change. They always said no.

So when I told them I'd be preaching one night, I didn't expect much. I'd told them before. I'd invited them before. And every time, they passed.

But this time, something changed. Maybe it was curiosity. Maybe they were just in a better mood. Maybe the drinking softened something in them that night. I still don't know. But they said yes.

And they came.

I almost didn't believe it when I saw them walk through the church doors—it didn't feel real.

Dear Red Straw

It was a cold, snowy Friday night—deep winter. My nerves were on fire. Not just because I was preaching, but because my parents were there.

Preaching—even when you've done it a bunch of times before—is an act of trust. You step up in front of a crowd with an idea, some notes scratched out on paper, but you're never fully sure how it'll go. You just hope for the right words to come to mind when you need them.

That night, walking up to the pulpit, I could feel it in my body—the nervous uncertainty building up.

I set my Bible down. Adjusted the mic. The church was quiet. Not calm—just awkward. Like everyone was waiting to see if I'd mess it up.

I wiped the sweat from my brow, looked down at my messy notes, and opened my mouth.

And I began to preach.

I preached about Job—a man who had everything. A good life. Wealth. Family. Stability. And then, just like that, he lost it all. Like someone living a quiet life in the countryside, never seeing the fire coming until everything's burned up.

Job lost his home, his health, his family—his whole world. He went through hell but never turned his back on God. And after all that suffering, everything he lost was given back to him.

I preached for over an hour—about perseverance, about trusting God through pain, about holding on when life strips everything away.

And my parents were there to see it.

But the moment I finished, they shook the pastor's hand and walked out like it was just another church service. We never talked about it. Not that night. Not after. They never said a word about the message. And I didn't ask. I think part of me was too afraid to hear what they really thought.

Did it change them? Did it save them from their drinking? Make them want to live differently?

No.

And that broke me.

I felt like I'd failed—failed them, failed God, failed myself. I blamed myself for not being able to save them.

But now I see it for what it was—that sermon wasn't for them. It was for the people in that church. The ones looking for hope. The ones trying to find a way out of whatever pain they were stuck in.

My parents weren't looking. They didn't think they needed help. And you can't save someone who doesn't want to be saved.

They already had what they needed. And what they needed... was alcohol.

It took me years to stop blaming myself. To stop thinking that if I'd just been a better preacher, a better son, a better Christian—I could've changed them.

But you can't make someone change.

They have to want it. They have to choose it.

Dear Red Straw

And until they did, there was nothing I could've done.

Jeremy Allen Damours

"I'm sorry…"

I said it all the time—way more than I needed to. I apologized so often, sometimes I didn't even know what I was apologizing for. It was just... automatic.

The older I got, the more I realized that guilt didn't go away just because I wasn't living at home anymore. It came with me—into conversations, into work, into everything.

Feeling the blame didn't just happen overnight. It built slowly, over years of living in a house where moods changed fast and people said things they shouldn't have. It wasn't just the mess—it was the way I was treated inside of it. I learned to take the blame for things that weren't mine.

I got good at reading the room, picking up on little things—like a slammed silverware drawer or a sudden change in tone—anything that might warn me about what was coming. If I could stay ahead of it, maybe I could stop things from getting worse. Maybe I could keep the peace.

I felt responsible for keeping everyone calm. And when my parents weren't happy—whether they were having a bad day or, in my case, when I managed to get them out of the house to do something different, like visit relatives, go to an event in town, or even show up to my high school graduation—I felt guilty.

I knew the second we left they were already counting the minutes until they could get back home to

Dear Red Straw

drink. So I started believing that if I could just keep them happy long enough, maybe we could enjoy ourselves like other families did. Maybe, just maybe, I could control what I couldn't fix.

My dad's moods were all over the place when he drank. One minute, he'd be sitting quietly at his desk, going over paperwork from his job—lost in it, like work was the only thing besides drinking that could hold his attention. And he was always working, even when he wasn't on the clock—lining things up, running numbers, sorting through piles of paper. His whole world was really just two things: getting drunk and working.

Then, out of nowhere, he'd drop something or snap over a comment one of us said that he didn't like. He'd slam his fists on whatever he could slam them on and yell, "God DAMNIT to hell!"—sometimes with no one's name attached at all. We'd sit there, quiet, hoping he'd calm down quickly. But that wasn't so easy. Once he got mad about something, he'd go on about it for hours.

Living like that—never knowing what would set him off—felt like walking on eggshells. I kept telling myself that if I could keep him calm, maybe nothing bad would happen. If I could keep the peace, maybe I could protect my mom, my brothers, and myself.

That kind of guilt doesn't just go away. It sinks in deep. After a while, it starts to feel normal—like you're always doing something wrong. And for a long time, I believed that.

At work, if someone dropped a pen near me, I'd say "I'm sorry" without even thinking. If I had to cancel plans or miss a family event, I'd feel sick with guilt—like I was letting everyone down and didn't deserve a second chance.

And if someone looked even a little upset, my mind would start spinning. Maybe they were already in a bad mood when the conversation started. Maybe I'd seen them get upset with someone else earlier, and now they were being a little rude with me—so I'd start wondering if I had done the same thing. Or maybe they were fine one minute and then cold the next. Either way, I'd start going over everything I said, right away, trying to figure out what I did wrong.

Every little thing started to feel like it was on me. Even stuff that had nothing to do with me felt like something I had to say sorry for.

It took getting away from all the stress and guilt I grew up with to finally see what was really going on. And even then, it took years to realize when I was doing it.

But now, I catch it more often. I remind myself that I don't owe anyone an apology just for being here.

And when I need the reminder, I tell myself, "You don't need to be sorry for this."

Dear Red Straw

When shame and guilt have always been there, they feel normal. We think everything's our fault, even when it clearly isn't. We blame ourselves for their moods, their unhappiness. Say sorry for things we didn't do. And hold on to feelings we should've never had to hold.

But shame and guilt don't stay in the past. They follow us into everything. They mess with how we see ourselves. They make us second-guess what we say, keep quiet when we want to speak up, and try to keep people happy even when we're falling apart inside.

I believed all of it for years. I thought if I worked harder, stayed out of the way, and kept everything under control, I'd finally feel okay. But it didn't matter what I did—because the truth is, none of it started with me.

Letting go of that guilt doesn't mean pretending it didn't happen. It means seeing their choices for what they were—and knowing they weren't our fault. It means remembering that we were just kids, doing our best to get through something confusing and messy. And it means giving ourselves a chance at living differently than the way we were raised.

The truth is, we're not stuck with the choices our parents made. We don't have to carry the mess they never dealt with. And we sure as hell don't have to keep saying sorry just for being here.

Real healing starts when we stop blaming ourselves. Shame and guilt might've helped us get by— kept us quiet, kept us careful, kept us out of the way.

Maybe we needed that back then. But we don't need it now.

We don't have to carry the guilt. We can let the shame go. And we can stop saying sorry for things we didn't cause and couldn't control.

The past might've taught us to feel small. But we don't have to keep living like that.

We can drop the weight. We can come up for air.

And for once, we can finally breathe.

Dear Red Straw

Dear Mom and Dad,

Do you remember that cold October night when I came home and knocked on your bedroom door to tell you I hit a moose on my way home? I don't think any of us have forgotten that night.

You were both lying in bed when I showed up. I was shaken, panicked, and still trying to process what had just happened. I thought I was a man at seventeen, but when that moose came out of nowhere and my car slammed into it—stopping instantly, like I'd hit a wall—I didn't feel like a man anymore. I was a scared kid who didn't know what to do. I needed you. I needed you to be sober. I needed you to comfort me, tell me everything was going to be okay, and make me feel like the world wasn't crashing down around me.

When you answered my knocks, the sound of your voices surprised me. They were sober. Familiar in a way I didn't usually hear at night. I didn't stop to question it—I just spilled everything. The crash, the fear, the shock of seeing that massive moose lying there in front of me on the road. I didn't know how you'd react, but you didn't seem mad. You didn't ask how bad the car was. You just wanted to know if I was okay. And that gave me something I didn't even realize I'd been craving: I finally felt like I had parents.

But what I didn't tell you that night was that I wasn't paying attention when I hit the moose. I'd just found out I was going to be a dad. My mind was completely somewhere else, stuck in this fog of "What the hell am I supposed to do now?" I didn't see the moose until it was too late. And part of me wondered if maybe that was some kind of sign—like the universe was telling me I was barreling toward a future I wasn't ready for.

It took me days to work up the courage to tell you about the pregnancy. And honestly, I probably never would have if Mom hadn't figured it out herself. You made some random guess, Mom, when you saw her eating saltine crackers and drinking 7-Up—and you were right. I was relieved you finally knew. I braced myself for what was

Dear Red Straw

coming—for the anger, the judgment, the shame. I expected you both to blow up, to say I'd ruined my life or let you down.

But you didn't.

You didn't get mad. You didn't lecture me. You didn't make me feel like I was worthless.

For all the times you weren't sober when I needed you... you were sober that time. And I needed it more than you'll probably ever know.

Thank you for that.

CHAPTER 5

AVOIDING THE STORM

Before trouble slips out of the shadows, something in you already knows.

A stranger watching a little too closely. A car beside you, slowly veering into your lane on a busy freeway. Dark clouds building overhead while you're out walking, miles from home.

Someone coming toward you with a smile that doesn't quite reach their eyes.

Still. Some things don't look wrong—but they still feel that way.

The gut feeling—that voice inside you that won't shut up. The one screaming not to go with that person, not to walk into that building, not to follow through with the plan in your head.

Some people trust that voice. They back out before things go too far. They drop the plan, change direction, or get out while it still feels safe.

Others ignore it. They keep going—telling themselves it's fine—until it isn't.

Do you trust that voice?

If you're lucky, you hear it in time. You stop short before things get bad.

But not everyone does. Some don't make it out. They stay too long. They live with whatever comes next.

That voice isn't random. It's there to protect you. And most of the time, it's right.

But when you grow up around alcoholism, your sense of danger gets warped. The threat isn't out in the world—it's right inside the place that's supposed to keep you safe.

You're learning what safe feels like from people who are lost in their own chaos.

When the ones taking care of us drink too much, we feel it. Their drinking—even if they don't mean to hurt us—becomes its own form of neglect. They might be in the room, but their minds are gone—lost in the bottle, lost in themselves.

And because they're not really there, we're left with too much to figure out on our own. No real conversations. No one to guide us. No one showing us how to handle things or helping us understand what's normal and what's not.

It doesn't always stop there. What starts as emotional pain turns into bruises. Someone gets slapped. Someone gets dragged by the arm. Sometimes its hair pulled or being shoved into a wall.

So, we become people-pleasers. We smooth things over. We do whatever we can to make things better—even if it means staying quiet, backing down, or pretending we're fine when we're not.

Dear Red Straw

After a while, it becomes automatic. We hold back with our partners. We stay quiet at work. We nod along even when we don't agree. We change the subject the second things get tense. And sometimes, we say yes to things we don't even want—just to avoid the stomach-turning dread that comes with speaking up.

Yeah, what we've been through is real. And it's messed with how we deal with stuff. But there's another side to it.

Not every storm is bad. It can bring up things that have been stuck for way too long. While it feels messy, it brings us closer. Gives us a chance to stop pretending, say what we mean, and hear each other out.

The problem is, when we spend our lives avoiding it, we start to resent the very people we're trying to protect. That resentment turns into distance. And that distance? It can end relationships that might've had a chance—if we'd just said what was really on our mind.

The storms we grew up with taught us to see conflict as danger. But those storms can be behind us now. And it's time to start hearing that voice inside differently—not as a warning to stay quiet, but as a push to speak up when something doesn't feel right.

Jeremy Allen Damours

I've brought it up to my mom over the years—how she and my dad raised us, with all the drinking and how unpredictable everything was. I try to be honest about how it affected us without being too hard on her. I don't want to pretend it wasn't that bad or act like she didn't have a part in it. But at the same time, I still feel the need to show her some understanding.

Like my brothers and me, she grew up around drinking and abuse. My mom never hit us, but the stuff she went through didn't just go away as an adult. And like me, she didn't realize how messed up her childhood really was until much later.

She and her sister lived through years of mayhem, but they didn't know it was unusual. To them, it was just normal.

My mom met my dad at fifteen and married him almost right away—not realizing she was trying to escape. She wouldn't see that part until a long time later. Her sister did the same thing: met a boy and got married at fifteen. That kind of pattern doesn't just happen for no reason.

They were surviving it, not seeing it—and already halfway out the door without realizing it.

They probably thought it was love—but I don't think that's why they got married. They wanted peace. They wanted to feel normal. They wanted some control over their lives. It felt like a way out.

Dear Red Straw

But instead of calm, my mom walked straight into another storm. She left one controlling situation for another. And this time, there would be no room for her to grow or figure out who she was.

The more I've thought about it over time, the more I've tried to see it for what it really was.

Could she have left my dad and stopped drinking to give us a better life growing up? Sure. That would've been fair to expect. But fair doesn't mean it was something she could actually do. She was stuck—mentally, money-wise, and in a life that kept her silent. And even when help offered itself, it wasn't the kind she wanted. It was too blunt. Too honest. Too much like a mirror she didn't want to look into.

It was easier for her to go along with his choices than to face everything on her own.

My dad's control over her—along with their drinking—was a mess that kept her trapped. One that most people couldn't just walk away from.

I don't know much about my dad's childhood. It never sounded as dark or chaotic as my mom's. If there was pain, he never talked about it. I'm sure he had his own stuff, but I don't think his drinking came from the same kind of hurt. It seemed more like something he leaned on—until it got too strong to put down.

If he had quit drinking, I'm convinced my mom would've stopped too.

The cycle didn't start with my parents. It was already there before they met.

Jeremy Allen Damours

My grandma Joyce was an alcoholic. My mom never sugarcoated that. Grandma didn't work outside the home, which let her hide just how bad things were. Inside the house, it was hard to ignore. Her moods were up and down, and she'd take it out on my mom and her sister—hitting, scratching, yanking hair. She'd snap over anything: a spilled drink, a towel left out, even them getting wet walking to school in the rain.

There was no warning. One second she seemed okay. The next, she was grabbing them.

Even family vacations weren't safe from her drinking. One night during a trip, grandma snuck out of the motel room after everyone had fallen asleep. Hours later, she came back and parked the car in a different spot. The front end was smashed in, and she never said where she'd gone or what had happened.

The next morning, when grandpa saw the car, he asked her about it—why the car was moved, why it was damaged. She just shrugged. No explanation. And he didn't say anything else. He never did.

He didn't ask again. He just went back to doing what he always did.

Instead of dealing with it, he disappeared into work. He was a phone company manager, gone before sunrise and home after dark. Even on weekends, when he didn't have to work, he'd find a reason to go in. And when he was home, he mostly slept on the couch—a quiet escape from everything that came with living in that house.

Dear Red Straw

But he wasn't just staying away from grandma. He was leaving my mom and her sister alone in it.

Grandma was good at hiding her drinking. Vodka was her choice, and she never left bottles out. She could cover it so well that even her close friends didn't notice. Neither did my mom—until the day she went to clean a cut with the hydrogen peroxide from the bathroom cabinet. When she tipped the bottle over a cotton ball, the clear liquid smelled… off. It wasn't peroxide. It was vodka.

Grandma had been swapping out the peroxide with vodka to keep a regular stash hidden in plain sight.

That's when it hit her: her mother wasn't just moody or up and down. She was an alcoholic.

Jeremy Allen Damours

It's strange how something can feel off, and you know it—but still, you convince yourself to brush it aside. I learned the cost of that the hard way, standing behind a teller window.

Not long after I turned eighteen, I got a job at a local credit union. I was nervous to apply, surprised when they called me in, and even more unsure when I said yes. The thought of dealing with angry people and their money terrified me. I don't even know why I applied. Maybe part of me just wanted to prove I could handle what scared me.

I was tired of running from anything that felt uncomfortable—arguments, pressure, people getting upset. I needed to prove to myself that I wasn't a coward—that I could face what scared me and deal with it. So I took the job, even though I didn't feel ready.

It didn't pay much—just $7 an hour. My boss had me go back and forth between the teller line and the drive-up window.

The drive-up made me uneasy. I was alone in a small room off to the side, with nobody around if something went wrong. But I also liked it. The bulletproof glass made me feel safer. If someone got angry, they could yell, but they couldn't do much more than that before driving off.

One afternoon, while I was working the teller line inside, a woman walked up to my window. Right away she made me nervous. She was impatient and in a

Dear Red Straw

rush, like she didn't want to give me time to catch on to what she was doing.

There was something about the way she kept looking over her shoulder, and the way she looked at me, that made me uneasy.

She glanced up at the ceiling toward the camera in the corner, then looked straight back at me and locked eyes. I looked down uncomfortably, hoping she'd stop, but she kept staring. She didn't break eye contact, even after I looked away.

I asked if she had her ID. I needed to know who she was. She didn't answer right away. Just kept staring. There was a heavy silence before she finally said no.

My chest started to tighten. My heart was beating faster, and it was getting harder to breathe. My hands were starting to sweat, and I could hear the shakiness in my voice. I tried to stay calm, but my muscles were too tense. Something was wrong. I just didn't know what yet.

She suddenly started speaking faster, her eyes darting around like someone was following her. She demanded one request after another—deposit this, withdraw that, cash this check.

I asked her to slow down and give me one thing at a time, but she ignored me and kept going. Her voice kept rising, louder and harsher, like she was trying to wear me down.

When she slid her check across the counter, she didn't ask me to cash it. She told me with her eyes. My heart was racing.

Jeremy Allen Damours

I knew the rule: no ID, no cash. But the way she looked at me was intense—like she was daring me to say no.

I asked for ID again, but she snapped that she was a regular and had cashed checks here without it before. Told me to trust her.

My stomach knotted. I didn't want to cause more of a scene, and I didn't want to make her any angrier.

Against my better judgement, I gave in. I cashed the check for five hundred dollars, handed her the money, and watched her shove it into her purse like she'd won something. Then she turned and walked out like I wasn't even there.

A month later, two police officers showed up and asked to speak to my manager. I was working the teller line when she called me into her office.

When I saw the officers, I knew. They handed me a copy of the check. It was stolen. The police asked for a description, but all I could think about was that moment at my window—how I knew better, and still gave in.

I backed down when it got tough. I didn't get fired, but my boss stopped trusting me. She didn't say it—but I knew. That's what it cost me.

Dear Red Straw

I wish I could say that was the last time I ignored my instincts. But years later, I did it again—backed down, ignored the part of me that knew better, and said yes when I wanted to say no.

I was in my thirties by then. I'd had time since the credit union incident to work on myself—time to go through a divorce, fall in love again, and start seeing some of the ways I was making things harder than they had to be. Michael helped with that. He didn't just love me; he challenged me.

I thought I was doing better—until my coworker Natalie came to me with a business opportunity.

She'd been hinting at it for months—making little comments after staff meetings or if we ran into each other in the copier room. Just enough to let me know she was involved in something life-changing and thought I'd be "good at it." I never asked what it was. I wasn't interested. I didn't want to start more talk about it. I figured she'd eventually tell me what it was really about.

One day, as I was leaving the office, Natalie handed me a business card for the life-changing thing she'd been talking about. Said she'd be sending me some links and would follow up after I watched the videos. So I gave her my email.

At the time, I didn't know anything about multi-level marketing—also known as pyramid schemes. I watched the videos that evening and realized they were trying to get me to sign up to sell night cream for wrinkles. It looked like it worked. The reviews were full of people raving about it.

They also promised a glamorous, flexible lifestyle—working from my phone, on the beach, anywhere in the world. They said if I got enough customers and brought in other people to sell with me, I could one day stop working altogether. Just sit back and collect money. There were promises of big bonuses, fancy titles, and even a free car.

But I'm not a salesperson. I hate the feeling of trying to talk people into buying things—especially people I know. It makes me feel like I'm crossing a line, like I'm asking for something I shouldn't be asking for. The whole thing just made me cringe.

When Natalie called that night, I tried to tell her no. Told her I wasn't a salesperson. That it made me uncomfortable. That I wasn't the kind of person who could do that, and I probably wouldn't be any good at it.

But she brushed it off like it didn't matter. Said I didn't need to be a salesperson—that the product would sell itself. All I had to do was hand it out and let people try it.

That would turn out to be a lie.

Still, her words got in my head. And I didn't want to let her down. So I gave in and joined the business with her.

It felt exciting at first. I had my own website. I was handing out samples, going to team meetings, trying to learn how to sell something I wasn't even sure I believed in yet.

But it didn't take long to see that none of it was working. People wanted the freebies—not the pricey cream.

I ran ads on social media. Threw little get-togethers, hoping friends would bring friends. I spent hours trying to make something happen. But the sales weren't coming. And most of the time, I was avoiding cold calls and dreading the thought of talking to strangers—because I hated confrontation.

And when someone finally did listen, they all said the same thing—it was too expensive.

I started feeling bitter—but not toward Natalie. I was mad at myself. For letting her talk me into something I wasn't sure about. For going along with it when deep down, I had doubts. For not speaking up.

I had gotten excited when people liked the samples. I wanted to believe it could work. But when the sales didn't come, and her promise that it would sell itself fell apart, I felt stupid for trusting it. I was worn out by my own inability to just say no.

I thought avoiding hard conversations would make things easier. But it ended up costing me time, money, and peace of mind.

Jeremy Allen Damours

That wasn't the first time I ignored what I needed, just to keep things from getting uncomfortable.

I started doing that when I was a kid. I needed to feel safe. I needed to speak up. But I didn't. I had already learned to stay quiet and not make things worse.

My dad's moods could be easy to read—until they weren't.

Some days, I knew what kind of mood he was in and stayed out of the way. Being able to read him made me feel like I had some control—like if I was careful enough, I could keep things from blowing up.

But that's what made it worse when he got angry. Just when I thought I had him figured out, he'd yell—and whatever sense of control I thought I had would disappear in seconds.

One Saturday morning, when my twin brother and I were about nine, we were playing quietly on the living room floor while my dad sat on the couch watching a movie. The house we were renting had a huge living room—so big it felt endless to us at that age.

Windows lined almost every wall except the one connected to the kitchen. The south side looked out over a wide valley—patches of forest and fields with a single road winding its way into town. If you followed that same road the other way, it kept going—through tiny villages, past Denali, and eventually all the way to Anchorage.

Dear Red Straw

The east windows looked out toward our neighbors and the thick woods that stretched out behind their land. In the summer, they raised and butchered chickens. In the fall, the smell of smoked salmon drifted through the trees.

The neighbor directly across the street had a massive dog named Wolfpack—part wolf. He looked feral, like he belonged to the wilderness, not a yard. But he was a gentle giant. He could sneak up so quietly you wouldn't hear a thing. You'd just turn around—and there he'd be, watching. If you didn't know he was friendly, you'd think he was about to drag you into the woods.

The north windows overlooked a makeshift junkyard where our landlord had stashed old cars, including an antique fire truck. It was an eyesore—except in winter, when heavy snow buried everything and made it disappear for the season.

The fire truck, though, didn't feel like junk to us. My brothers and I spent summers climbing all over it, turning the wheel, pressing invisible buttons, and pretending we were racing off to save someone.

Most of our time, though, we were inside, trying to stay warm through the long winters. The living room was where we made the best memories in that house. It was the one place where we actually spent time together as a family.

But that sense of safety shattered one Saturday morning.

My brother and I were playing quietly. We knew how easily our dad could snap when there was too much noise. When he got mad, his whole face would twist up, like he was getting ready to blow. His teeth would start to grind, and then—like always—he'd shout his usual "GOD DAMMIT!" before tearing into whatever set him off.

But this morning would be different.

We were keeping to ourselves—no running, no yelling, no bothering him. Just doing everything we knew to do. And still, something set him off.

One second, we were playing, and the next, he was standing over us.

Even now, I still don't know what set him off. I've tried to figure it out, but maybe there was nothing to figure out. He hadn't been drinking, which somehow made it worse—because there was no excuse, no warning, nothing we could blame it on.

His face twisted up—meaner than I'd ever seen. His teeth started to gnash. And then it came.

"GOD DAMMIT!"

"What's wrong with you!"

"I told you to stop it!"

What was he even talking about? What was wrong with us? What were we supposed to stop doing? I don't remember much else he said—because I couldn't stop staring at something else.

He was frozen—too full of rage to move. A thick string of phlegm dangled from his mouth, stretching and thinning, then splitting into two, then three, swaying

Dear Red Straw

between his clenched teeth as he kept gnashing, like some rabid animal.

My mom rushed over, gently pushing him back toward the kitchen, trying to defuse whatever was happening before it got worse.

My brother and I just stared at each other, too stunned to speak. We were scared—but more than anything, confused.

We had been playing quietly. Minding our own business. We hadn't done anything to set him off.

Even now, I still don't know why he reacted that way.

But I remember what I saw in his eyes—something I'd never seen before.

Hollowness.

Like his soul had left the room, and all that was left was raw, burning rage.

Not aimed at me. Not aimed at my brother.

Just there—spilling out, and we were in the way.

It was hard to look at my dad the same way after that. I kept replaying the moment, trying to figure out what I had done to make him so angry. When I couldn't find an answer, I stopped looking. I started accepting the possibility that maybe it had nothing to do with me at all. Maybe he was just angry at everything.

Or maybe he was angry that I was here in a world he didn't want me to be in.

Jeremy Allen Damours

It didn't matter if I caused it or not. The storm still came. So I just got more careful. Watched more. Spoke less.

Dear Red Straw

I learned early how to keep things from turning into a fight, even when I should've spoken up.

I dragged that with me into friendships, into work, into love.

I didn't know how to talk about what was bothering me. I held it in until it boiled over. And early on with Michael—the man I'd end up building a life with—that habit came out like I was trying to push him away, even though I wasn't.

Being an adult is hard enough with work and bills—but it's even harder when the people you care about don't feel like they can tell you what's really going on. Friends, lovers, coworkers—something seems off, but they're afraid to say anything. They feel left out, take something the wrong way, or stay quiet. And while it's building up, they're pulling away, their attitude gets worse, and they start snapping over small things.

I used to think it was better to just keep quiet. I didn't want to upset anyone, so I kept things to myself—even when they were bothering me. But staying quiet doesn't fix anything. The relationship doesn't get better—it just starts to fall apart. You stop talking about what matters, and after a while, there's nothing holding it together.

Growing up around alcohol, I learned really quick that bringing things up caused problems. If my parents had been drinking, it would start with slurred fights—just the same things repeated over and over—and end with someone walking out. And if they weren't drinking, my dad would shut down. My mom would try to go back and forth between us, trying to fix it, but by then he wasn't saying anything. And we kids would go quiet too. Nothing ever got worked out. We didn't want the drunken fights or the silence that came after.

But that doesn't work when you're trying to build something that lasts. Michael grew up in a home where saying what was on your mind wasn't a big thing. You said it, talked it out, and moved on.

His childhood wasn't without its own problems, but it was calm compared to mine. So when we got close, it was only a matter of time before the way I handled things and the way he did started to clash.

And one night, I lost it.

We weren't living together yet, but we might as well have been. I walked into his place like I always did—dropped my stuff by the door, kicked off my shoes, and asked, "What've you been up to today?"

Just making conversation. But really, I was waiting for him to bring it up. Why I wasn't there. Why I hadn't been invited.

He said he spent the day with his mom, grandparents, and some cousins who were visiting from out of town. That was it. He just said it like it was normal. Like there was nothing weird about me not being there.

We were both off that day. Normally, we'd spend the whole day together. But I hadn't heard from him until that evening, and now I was just sitting there,

Dear Red Straw

pretending everything was fine while he talked like nothing was wrong.

I stayed quiet, waiting for him to say something that would explain it—even just a little. But he didn't.

He kept talking about lunch, about his cousins, about nothing. I nodded along, trying to look fine, but it was already getting to me.

I hadn't been invited. And what stung more was that he didn't seem to care.

He knew I was off. He knew we were serious. So what was I supposed to do—just sit there and act like it didn't matter?

I didn't ask him about it. Didn't say a word. I was scared of what he'd say—scared he'd get mad or think I was blowing it out of proportion.

So I held it in.

And the longer I did, the heavier it sat on me. I gave short answers, stared at the floor, barely looked at him. Every time he asked what was wrong, I said, "Nothing."

But it wasn't nothing. It was all of it.

Later, after he fell asleep on the couch, I got up and started throwing things. Not at him—just around the room. Loud enough to wake him up. Loud enough to say I wasn't okay—without having to say it out loud.

He woke up confused. I was already in the middle of losing it.

I started yelling—not even sure what I was saying. It all came out scrambled, like I'd been holding it in too long to say it right.

That's when he told me something I didn't know.

He'd already fought with his mom that day. Told her I was part of his life now. Told her she didn't get to leave me out. Said it got so bad, she cried. He hadn't said anything to me because he didn't have it in him to go through it all again. He'd already stood up for me once—and now he just wanted a quiet night.

I knew I'd blown it.

I stood there feeling awful—realizing I had made him the bad guy when he'd been standing up for me, and I'd turned him into the enemy.

All because I didn't know how to just say what was wrong.

That's when it hit me. I was still holding on to all the old stuff. And I was putting it on him too.

The way I'd handled things growing up wasn't working anymore. Not with someone like Michael—someone who actually wanted to talk things through, even if not every moment was the right one. If I wanted to keep him in my life, I had to start being honest. Speak up more. Stop acting like everything was fine when it wasn't.

That night didn't fix me. But it showed me that not every hard conversation has to end in yelling—or silence. That not everything has to turn into a fight. That sometimes, the hardest part isn't saying what's wrong—

it's trusting that someone will still love you after you do.

Jeremy Allen Damours

The storms we grew up in shaped the way we move through the world. When home was unpredictable—when the people who were supposed to protect us were the ones we had to protect ourselves from—we learned how to keep the peace.

We got good at reading moods. Figuring out what version of someone was walking through the door. Smoothing things over before they blew up.

And when we couldn't stop the storm, we just waited for it to hit.

That reaction—to make ourselves easy to be around and not cause problems—helped us survive. But it came at a cost.

We learned that hard moments weren't safe. That asking for what we needed might lead to yelling, getting pushed away, guilt trips, or someone walking out. So we didn't ask. We kept quiet. We tried not to need anything at all.

But silence doesn't fix anything. It builds. It eats at us. And after a while, it starts to show—through distance, tension, resentment, outbursts we didn't see coming. Sometimes, it ends the very relationships we were trying so hard to hold onto.

And the worst part? The problem isn't the conflict itself. It's how afraid of it we learned to be.

It took me a long time to see that. That not every problem is a threat. That not everyone is going to explode or walk away. That conflict, in the right kind of relationship, isn't something to be afraid of—it's something to work through.

The storms we grew up in trained us to avoid conflict at all costs. But we're not living in that storm anymore.

If we want real relationships—ones that last—we have to stop avoiding and start showing up. We have to speak up, set boundaries, say what's true. Even when it's uncomfortable.

Avoiding the storm may have kept us safe back then.

But facing it now? That's what sets us free.

Jeremy Allen Damours

Dear Mom and Dad,

I was so excited when I bought our plane tickets to come and see you both for Christmas that year. Mom, even though you were the one I spoke to on the phone in the months leading up to our visit, it felt like you and Dad were actually doing well for a change. You didn't sound drunk when I called, and for once, it seemed like maybe, just maybe, things were on a positive path. I let myself believe that.

I was especially excited to bring Michael and the boys and stay in your cabin by the Chena River. I couldn't wait to have a snowy Christmas together as a family. After all, it had been years since we had seen each other.

It seemed like things were going well when we got to Alaska. You welcomed us at the airport late that night, the air so sharp and cold that it took my breath away. Snow was piled high on the roads, and I had almost forgotten what it felt like to be back in an

Dear Red Straw

Alaskan winter until that trip brought it all rushing back. I remember trailing behind you in the rental car, gripping the wheel tightly, following your taillights as we crawled down the icy roads. It felt like driving on glass. But muscle memory kicked in, and soon, I remembered how to move with the snow instead of against it.

But when we got back to your place and I watched you both pour your drinks, the excitement I had been holding onto wavered. I felt disappointed, but I suppressed it. I told myself I wouldn't let your drinking ruin the trip. I wanted this Christmas to be different. I wanted us to be together as a family. I wanted to ignore the alcohol, to pretend like it didn't exist, even if it was in plain view.

The next day shattered that illusion. I should have known better.

That afternoon, I had a wonderful time catching up with Shany at the coffee shop. It had been years since we had seen each other, and for just a few hours, I let myself exist in a world outside of family responsibilities. I never meant to be gone so long, but our conversation stretched into the evening, time slipping away in a way it never does when you are with someone who truly understands you. In my mind, I was only asking for a few hours to myself, just a few hours out of an entire seven day trip. Was that really too much to ask?

Apparently, it was.

I should have known better than to leave Michael and the boys alone with you for that long. I should have remembered that Dad gets suspicious when he is drunk. I should have remembered that to Michael, the way I was raised was completely foreign. I should have thought about the boys and how unfamiliar all of this would be to them. But I didn't. I let myself believe, just for a little while, that I could trust you to hold things together.

I was wrong.

Dad, you were irate when I got home. You couldn't let it go. You turned my afternoon with a friend into something about you. You ranted, pacing, accusing me of being out with Shany to plan an intervention to save you from your alcoholism.

The only silver lining was that, for once, you were acknowledging your addiction. Because why else would you even suspect an intervention?

But what hurt the most, what frustrated me beyond words, was how you wouldn't believe me. No matter how many times I told you, over and over again, that I had simply been catching up with a friend, you refused to hear me. You were too drunk, too far gone, too caught up in your own paranoia. You couldn't see that I had stopped trying to save you a long time ago.

I had already made peace with the fact that I couldn't fix you.

I didn't tell you that I had accepted, years ago, that alcohol had more of a hold on you than I ever could. I didn't tell you that my only goal in coming was to spend whatever time I had left with you before the drinking took what little was left of you.

But none of that mattered in that moment. You were set on making a scene, and you did, right in front of Michael and the boys. The air in the house became thick and suffocating, and I felt the overwhelming urge to leave. I started searching for motels. I would have packed up and gone that night if Mom and Michael hadn't stopped me, convincing me to stay.

"We came here to be together," they said. "To spend Christmas as a family."

I gave in. But only after Mom finally calmed you down and put you to bed.

The trip was never the same after that.

You had ruined it. Again.

You were the storm I had been trying to outrun. And once again, I had let myself believe I was safe, only to be caught in it all over again.

CHAPTER 6

BLURRED LINES

Where do we end and others begin?

When there are no boundaries at home, the person drinking takes up all the space—so your needs get pushed aside.

Are we our own people, or just add-ons to the ones we were always trying to keep from falling apart?

Do we get to say what's okay and what's not—or is our worth based on how much we can give?

In a home where drinking came first, I'm not sure I ever learned the answer.

When drinking takes over, boundaries don't just get blurry—they disappear. We don't get to just be kids. We become whoever we need to be to keep things from turning into a mess.

We take on their moods. Their guilt. Their hurt. We bend ourselves to fit what they need, until we don't even know who we are without them.

That's what happens when boundaries disappear—things don't just get confusing. You start to disappear, too.

At first, it feels like being strong—being the one who keeps things together. But over time, it wears you down. You don't know how to say no, because it feels selfish. You think it's your job to fix how other people feel because no one ever taught you that you were allowed to have limits.

It took me a long time to stop thinking no was a bad word. That looking after myself doesn't mean I don't care. It just means I'm allowed to. And if I ever want to feel like a real person, I have to figure out where I end and everyone else begins.

But first, I had to let go of the idea that being useful was the same as being worthy.

Dear Red Straw

Sometimes, it starts with just one moment—one memory that sticks. Something small that tells you no one's really watching out for you. And after that, you start to feel like it's your job to keep everything together, even when it shouldn't be.

It was a warm summer evening. Dusk was just settling over the small trailer park where we lived, out in the Arizona desert. I was five years old, playing in the backyard by myself, watching some baby brown lizards jump across an old dried-up branch that had fallen from the ash tree.

It sat halfway in the dirt—its fat end buried in the dry ground, skinny end sticking up and poking through the chain-link fence that separated our yard from the neighbor's.

I crouched down near the branch, watching them leap from one side to the other. I kept thinking about how fast they were. What were they jumping for? Where were they trying to go? Did they live in the dirt, or had they fallen from the ash tree? Were they chasing ants? Hiding from something?

I didn't know. But I couldn't stop watching them.

As the minutes passed by, I looked up. It was getting harder to see. The light had changed. That soft purple sky was fading, and I could barely make out the dirt or the branch.

Suddenly, something felt off.

Jeremy Allen Damours

I looked back at the house. It was too quiet. You could usually hear everything from the backyard—parents talking, the TV, someone moving around. But that night, there was nothing. Just silence. Strange silence. My brothers were inside, but they were quiet too. Still, the house felt empty.

I knew something wasn't right. I ran inside to look for my parents, but nothing. My mom, who was always home—never went anywhere without us—wasn't there. Neither was Dad.

I walked out to where the car was always parked and saw the old station wagon sitting in the driveway. It had brown paneling on the sides and was long and square around the edges. It rode smooth, and my dad always kept it washed and polished.

The car was there, but they weren't.

For a second, I thought maybe they were next door. They had friends there—people they partied with. But something about it didn't feel right.

I walked over and pressed my hand to the hood.

It was warm.

That made it worse.

If it was warm, they had been here. But they were gone now. They'd come home—and left again. Without saying anything. Without taking us.

My heart started to pound. I could feel my legs beginning to shake. My head was filling with questions I didn't have answers to. Where did they go? Why didn't they tell us? Were they coming back?

Dear Red Straw

I just stood there, staring at the car, wishing it would tell me something. It didn't make any sense.

And then I thought about us.

Who was going to take care of us? What about my brothers? What if someone came while they were gone? What if something bad happened and no one even knew we were here?

I didn't know what to do. I felt like no one was coming.

And then—blinding headlights.

I didn't move. I wasn't thinking about running. I wasn't thinking at all. The fear just gripped me still.

I stood there squinting, trying to make out who it was. Through the glare, I could see three silhouettes sitting in the front seat of a big pick-up truck.

The door opened, and my dad jumped out first. My mom scooted across the seat and hopped down after him.

Relief, like waking up from a scary dream. That feeling in my chest—the panic—suddenly gone. I could breathe again. I wanted to cry. I wanted to run to them. But something held me back. I just stood there, like I wasn't sure they were really there.

I didn't know what I was expecting. But it wasn't this.

They were laughing. Smiling. Like nothing had happened. Like they hadn't just been gone. Like they hadn't left us without a word.

They saw me standing there.

But they didn't say anything. Didn't ask what I was doing outside. Didn't ask if I was okay. Didn't say where they'd been.

They just went inside—still laughing, still in their own world.

I stayed where I was.

I thought maybe one of them would turn around. Say something. Notice.

But they didn't.

Something changed in me right there. I didn't know if I could count on them to notice anymore.

I didn't have the words for it, but I felt it. The line between parent and kid—who's supposed to take care and who's supposed to be taken care of—suddenly didn't feel so clear.

I had never really questioned if my parents would be there. I hadn't thought about whether I was safe. That night was the first time I felt alone.

And the thing about feeling all alone is—when it happens once, it feels wrong. But if it keeps happening, it starts to feel normal.

When the people who are supposed to protect you don't…

When your needs are pushed aside…

You start to believe they don't matter.

And eventually, you stop thinking you're allowed to have them.

Dear Red Straw

A couple years later, on a frozen December's eve, we landed in Alaska. And for a while, it felt like the kind of magic any kid would dream of—snow falling, Christmas lights glowing, all of us tucked into that big log house like the past hadn't figured out where we were—yet.

I didn't know someone would ruin it so fast with a few careless words.

I was seven years old, and it was the second time I'd ever seen snow—real snow. But this time, I was going to live in it. It was everywhere—piled high along the roads, spread out across the fields, resting on the trees like frosting.

We were staying with my aunt and uncle until we could find a place of our own. Everyone kept talking about the cold—how it had hit seventy-five below zero and broken some kind of record.

The sting of the cold didn't bother us—maybe because school shut down for a few days. We just stayed inside, drinking hot chocolate under our blankets, the windows fogging up while the wind howled outside.

Then the monkey bread came out of the oven.

I'd never had anything like it back in Arizona. The smell hit you the second you walked through the door—thick and sweet, like butter and brown sugar was baking in the walls. Cinnamon floated in the air and settled into everything, making the whole place feel warmer, safer somehow. My aunt would pull it out of the oven in sticky, golden piles, still steaming. Each piece tugged away from the next like it couldn't wait to be eaten.

We'd tear it apart with our hands and eat it right off the tray, sticking to our fingers like syrupy glue. The outside was caramelized and crunchy. The inside, soft and gooey. We'd go back for more, licking our fingers between pieces.

As good as it all was, nothing felt quite like the night we waited for Santa.

We were all piled into the living room—me, my brothers, our cousins—laughing too loud, eating candy, and trying to stay awake long enough to hear reindeer land on the roof.

I remember thinking that even though we were hoping to see Santa and his reindeer, I didn't really believe it would happen. It never had before.

I had barely finished the thought when someone shouted they saw something—a red light, glowing outside. We all stopped moving, leaning in to listen. Could it be Rudolph?

Within seconds, we were running down the hall toward one of the bedrooms, all of us crowding around the window—elbows flying, breath fogging up the glass. It felt like we really were at the North Pole, waiting for Santa's sleigh to show up any second.

We pressed our noses against the glass, looking out at the yard for any hint of movement. The backyard stretched out forever—snow-covered hills, dark trees, nothing but untouched wilderness in sight. We stared

Dear Red Straw

into the night, waiting for something to break the stillness.

Beyond the hills, there were no houses. No roads. Just open land and thick silence. The moon lit up the trees along the ridge—bent, brittle pines twisted by the permafrost. They didn't look like trees to me. They looked like shadow beasts with tall, lanky bodies and spindly fingertips. Haunting, but not scary. Like they were part of the land—ancient things that watched but didn't move.

As we sat there, hushing each other, our eyes darted in every direction. Then we heard something above us.

Thud. A scuffle. Then silence.

We jumped up screaming—Santa had landed!

Then we saw it—a faint red glow bouncing off the trees, like it was coming from the roof.

We pressed our faces harder against the glass. Was it moving? Floating above us? Was it Rudolph, standing watch while Santa dropped through the chimney?

We sat there, quiet and still, barely breathing—sure we were just seconds away from seeing him.

But then... nothing. Minutes passed. Then a few more.

We ran to tell our parents what had happened, pulling them to the window and pointing out into the dark. But by the time they looked, the red light was gone. Santa must've realized we were still awake, they

Jeremy Allen Damours

said, so he'd have to come back later—once we were asleep.

I didn't need to see Santa to believe. I knew what I saw.

That night, I laid awake for what felt like hours, my heart pounding, replaying it all over and over.

The magic was real. I felt it.

But magic doesn't last forever.

Two years had gone by since that night. It was one of those warm summer evenings when everything felt still.

We were living in a place of our own now, away from our aunt and uncle and cousins. My parents used to take walks in the evenings, down the dusty dirt road that ran out from our house—the one that led to a trail that curved around a big open field.

That night, they asked us to go on a walk with them. We didn't know it would end the way it did.

As we walked, the ice in their cups tapped gently against the glass—soft and clinky, a scattered ting… tinga-ting… tingaling… ting… tingaling.

My dad carried his drink in his left hand, sipping through that same skinny red straw he always used. Bright red. Long. No bend.

He had no idea I was watching him.

He wrapped his lips around the tip of the straw—like he didn't want to let it go. Like he was shutting everything else out. The second he latched on, his eyes closed. And there it was—that look. Quiet.

Dear Red Straw

Still. Like something in him finally let go. Like he'd found the one thing that made him feel okay.

Four deep pulls. Slow. Rhythmic.

Each one timed just right—his throat bobbing with every swallow. It looked like something he'd done a million times, and it wasn't sloppy. I could almost feel him counting.

With the last swallow, his eyes stayed closed. Lips still pressed around the straw. He didn't move—just stayed there for a second, like he was deciding if he really wanted it to be over.

Then slowly, he let go.

He brought the cup back down, eyes open now, still wearing that look of quiet peace. A look I never saw him wear any other time in his life.

My mom drank too, but not like him. No straw. No pattern. Just a quick swig, like she wanted it over with. Her drinking was about getting it down, not making it last.

We were almost home—the house right there in front of us—when my dad, drunk and careless, suddenly blurted out:

"Santa Claus isn't real."

It hit me like a punch to the gut.

What?

No warning. No lead-up. Not even a conversation about Christmas.

Jeremy Allen Damours

It wasn't winter. It wasn't even close. Why was Santa on his mind? Why would he say that—so blunt, so mean—out of nowhere?

I felt a deep sadness in my chest. A kind of loss I didn't have words for. Santa wasn't just about presents. Santa was hope.

Santa meant something magical was still out there. Something to look forward to. Something safe. Something that never let you down.

He was one of the only things that never changed in my childhood, and my dad had erased him with a single sentence.

Then came the rest.

"And by the way... no Easter Bunny. No Tooth Fairy either."

He took another four long pulls through his red straw, the ice shifting as he lowered the cup.

I didn't know what to say. So I said nothing.

It wasn't just about Santa. Or losing the magic too soon.

It was about how there were no lines with him—not with feelings, not with personal stuff, not even the kind of basic things adults should keep to themselves. My dad didn't think about how we would feel. He just said it—quick and careless, like it didn't matter. Like he was talking about the weather.

That's how it always was. Just blurred lines all the time.

Dear Red Straw

When my dad died, I thought it would be the push my mom needed to clean up her life. She had spent so many years hiding behind him, it was easy to miss how bad things were with her too. But once he was gone, she couldn't blend hers with his anymore.

The blurred lines with my father? They didn't go away. They came back stronger. And this time, it was me and her.

As soon as he was gone, my mom moved in with Michael and me. She wasn't doing well enough to live on her own—not with how she was falling apart, and not with how bad things were with money.

For forty-five years, my mom had been controlled by the man she married at fifteen. She wasn't allowed to make choices for herself—couldn't get a license, couldn't decide where to go or when. My dad made every decision. She didn't question it. She just lived that way.

In some ways, her new beginning didn't feel like losing a husband. It felt more like an inmate being released after a lifetime inside.

What did she know about life outside that prison? Almost nothing.

The truth is, she never grew up. My dad didn't want her to. That was part of his control. She lived by his rules because she had to. And as the drinking got worse, she stopped thinking for herself completely. By the time she came to live with me, it was like looking after a teenager—angry, reckless, and out of control.

That's what she was starting with—years of mess and no clue what to do without him. And now I was the one stuck with what he left behind.

But I wasn't afraid of speaking up anymore. That part of me was done.

The hard part was honesty.

I didn't say certain things when I thought it might hurt her. I'd act like her choices weren't a big deal—even when they were. I didn't want to make anything worse—she was already trying to get through losing my dad and figure herself out.

So I made it seem like it didn't matter as much. I let things pass. Especially when it came to the decisions she was making. I told myself I was protecting her. But really, I just didn't want to add to her pain.

Now I see honesty isn't just about saying what's true—it's about saying what really needs to be said. Even when it's hard. Even when you know it might hurt. That's how you make it clear what's okay and what's not. And when we hold back from that, we're not helping anyone. We're just pretending it's fine when it's not.

One of the hardest times I had to be honest with my mom was when she started dating again.

After he died, she started seeing other men. Most of them were controlling and pushy. Sweet at first, then nasty.

Dear Red Straw

Jarvis was her first.

Jarvis worked in the hospital kitchen. My mom had been admitted for a procedure, and he was the one who brought her meals. He'd roll the cart by her room to deliver her tray, adjust her bed, fix the table height, and ask if she needed anything moved. He seemed into her right away.

He started making sure his route included her floor every day so he could see her. He told her he was a religious man, and I think that gave him a polished feel my mom thought she could trust.

After a few visits, he typed his number into her phone himself.

I don't think my mom was ever truly interested in Jarvis. I think she just wanted attention—any kind. Not because she was looking for love, but because she was trying to fill the space my dad left behind.

At first, he was a nice guy. But that didn't last long.

He started talking down to her and trying to boss her around. If my mom didn't want to go somewhere with him or changed plans, he'd get mad. If she told him no, he'd guilt-trip her or get moody.

He kept trying to get her to have sex. Every time they saw each other, he wanted more than she was okay with. Sometimes even in public.

"Stupid bitch," he'd say, when she wouldn't give him oral.

Jeremy Allen Damours

He loved telling her he was a man of God—but used that to get what he wanted.

That's what he'd say when she told him no—"God wants us to enjoy each other." Or, "I pray for you every day." He used faith as an excuse. Not to get close to her, but to control her. He didn't care about her soul. He just wanted her body.

Still, my mom kept going out with him. And every time, she'd end up wishing she hadn't.

She'd call me after—upset, embarrassed, sometimes even mad at herself.

"What do I do?" she'd ask. "He's not even nice to me."

"He keeps asking me to go sit in the park, but I know what he really wants. I don't want to, but he won't listen."

Then she'd say she was done. That she was blocking him. That she didn't want to see him again.

And then, a couple days later—she'd unblock him.

He'd call. She'd answer. He'd ask to see her. And she'd say yes.

And it would start all over again.

Each time, I told her the same thing. Stop seeing him. Listen to your gut. The way you feel around him isn't nothing—it means something.

But I always said it too nicely. I was careful. Too careful. What I should've said was: He's using you. He

Dear Red Straw

doesn't care about you. You're not safe with him. And you know it.

I didn't want to come off too mean, because I felt like I'd be the bad guy if she didn't take it well. Would it make her mad? Would it hurt her? Would it crush her?

And honestly, it wasn't just about her feelings. I was just plain tired.

I didn't want to keep getting dragged in again. I didn't want to argue when she didn't want to hear it. She kept making the same mistakes, and I kept saying the same thing—and nothing changed.

But part of me still believed I had to shield her from how she felt. Like if I said, "You can't keep doing this," I'd be saying, "You're on your own."

That's what happens when the lines are blurry. You stop being yourself and start being whatever keeps them from falling apart, even if it means you do.

Jeremy Allen Damours

After Jarvis, I hoped things would calm down for a while. That maybe the worst of it was over. But somehow, the drinking always came back and caused more problems.

It had been two years since my dad died, and my mom was relapsing again.

She had already been through rehab twice since he passed. Now she was back in for a third time.

At first, I was hopeful. I thought maybe this time, she'd finally stop digging herself deeper with the bottle and the men.

But then, while she was still in rehab, she started telling me about Glen—a man she'd met there.

At first, it was nothing—just a name she mentioned during a phone call. Someone she met in one of the group meetings.

But with every call, she started sharing more.

It started out with small things—how Glen was nice, how he checked on her during the day when they weren't in group.

Then it started to get more personal. He'd bring her food, sit with her during meals, and rub her back to ease her pain.

She couldn't stop talking about how sweet he was, how much he cared about her. Said the nurses were hitting on him. He was good-looking, smooth, the kind of guy who knew how to charm women and get noticed.

Dear Red Straw

She liked that he wanted her. He treated her like she was important.

But I didn't believe it. It was too perfect—too much, too fast. And coming from a man she'd just met in rehab, something felt off.

Then came the story. She kept telling it like it was the truth, even though it was full of holes.

His wife had died—in his arms, he said. But the story kept changing. One time, she died suddenly. Another time, she'd been sick for years. Sometimes he said he was there when it happened. Other times, he wasn't.

When I asked how she died, my mom hesitated—because he never really said. Every story was a little different. A little off. Like a puzzle with missing pieces.

Then there was his house. He said he owned it outright. But after he went into rehab, his own family moved in and told him it was theirs now. Took over like squatters—moved in while he was gone and planned to stay.

He kept saying he was going to deal with it when he got out, in about a month. People were in his house who weren't supposed to be, and he was going to wait that long to do something about it. It just didn't add up.

There was also his truck. He'd left it in a bar parking lot the day he went into rehab. Now he wasn't sure if it was still there, if it would be there when he got out, or even where it might end up.

But she didn't seem to doubt him. She just went along with what Glen told her—that people were taking things from him, doing him wrong, like he was the one being hurt.

He talked like he had nowhere to go and nothing to drive. He didn't seem worried about getting either one back. That's when it stopped making sense. Maybe there was never a house. Maybe there was never a truck.

By the time my mom got out of rehab, she was coming back to stay with me. And things with Glen had already gotten serious—at least in her mind. Glen was still in rehab, but they were on the phone all the time. He'd already talked her into going on a date with him once he got out—even though she lived more than 100 miles away.

That's when it hit me.

They were making plans. The rehab was going to give him a one-time-only ride—more than 100 miles—just to drop him off at a motel to meet my mom. They didn't know it was for a date. Didn't know it wasn't where he lived. That wasn't their job to question.

What about his truck? His house? How was he going to get back home?

And she was going along with it.

The more she talked about him, the more uneasy I felt. Not just because of him—but because of what might come next. What if he got stuck down here? What if things didn't work out, and she tried to bring him back to my place? What if she ran off with him for good? It felt like trouble waiting to happen.

Dear Red Straw

And then the day came. Glen was getting out, and my mom stood in the hallway zipping up her bag. I watched her walk out the door to meet him at the motel. I felt sick. I knew it wasn't going to end well. And I knew there was nothing I could do to stop it.

The house was quiet after she left. She didn't call. She didn't give me the address of where she was staying. For a while, I didn't hear anything—and I didn't mind. The place finally felt normal again. I hadn't realized how much she'd been wearing me down until she was gone.

But as the days passed, the silence started to feel different. I found myself wondering where she was, how things were going, whether she was safe.

And just as that worry started to settle in, she called.

There was no hello. No how are you. Just blurted it out:

"I need $400 right now or he's going to get mad at me!"

She sounded desperate—but not scared. Like she thought I'd just do it without asking why.

I was done. Everything in me said no.

I'd given her money before. Every time, I told myself I was helping. That she needed it. That I was doing the right thing.

But right then, I didn't feel like her son. I felt like an ATM. A transaction. Just a way to get what she wanted.

I asked what was going on. She wouldn't say. I asked why she needed the money. She wouldn't answer. I offered to come get her, to pay for her ride home, to get her out of whatever mess she was in.

She said no.

She didn't want help. She just wanted the money.

So for the first time, I said no.

I could hear the upset in her voice, but my decision was firm.

And then she did exactly what I knew she would do.

She called my brothers.

Then Michael.

Then my aunt.

Then old family friends.

After everyone said no, she called me back, hoping I'd give in.

But I didn't.

It hurt. Saying no felt like turning my back on her. Like I was abandoning her. I knew she had no money. I knew she was with the wrong person. But I couldn't do it anymore. I wasn't going to be another person she kept using.

For days, the guilt ate away at me. Had I just left my mom stuck? Had I given up on her?

Dear Red Straw

But then I reminded myself: If she was really in trouble, she would've said yes when I offered to come get her. She wasn't looking for help. She just wanted money.

And for the first time, I didn't give it to her. It was the first time I set a boundary with my mom—and actually held it.

She spent two weeks at that motel. When she asked if Glen could stay with me, I said no. I didn't give her any money. I stopped letting her use me. And when she came back, I never heard about Glen again.

Setting a boundary once isn't enough. You have to stay firm. And for the first time, I did.

Jeremy Allen Damours

As I continued setting small boundaries in my life, I started thinking about my dad. I never really got closure. I wondered where he was. If he was okay. If there was an afterlife. If we could still talk somehow.

I've always been curious about psychics. Never really doubted they were real. But when I was nineteen and started going to a Pentecostal church, I was told to stay away from them. They're dangerous, they'd preach from the pulpit. Called them sorcerers. Sinners. People you shouldn't go near. And during that time, I believed it.

After I left the church, the idea of seeing a psychic came back. I was still thinking about my dad. But I also needed to know if I was on the right path in life. I couldn't trust the church anymore. I needed something else. I wasn't looking for a new religion. I just wanted to feel connected to something again.

When I found out that my twin brother had gone to see a psychic medium in California, I was curious. He said a lot of our family members came through—talking through the psychic, one after another. The more he shared about what happened during his visit, the more I wanted to go too. Not just to see if the guy was real, but to see if I could walk away with my own answers.

When I showed up at Bill Philipps' office, I was tense. I didn't know what I was walking into. I was nervous about what might happen, who might come through, or what they might say. I was scared I'd leave with nothing. That it would all be a waste.

Dear Red Straw

I didn't tell Bill, but I had made a list of questions on a piece of paper and kept it hidden in my pocket. Things I was hoping he'd answer. Like: Where's my dad? Is he okay? Did Nathaniel die peacefully? What's my purpose in life? What should I be doing with my time on earth? What's my calling?

Bill gave me a hug like we already knew each other. I sat down next to him on the couch, the folded paper still tucked deep in my pocket.

And the reading began.

Almost immediately, they started coming through—one after another.

Both of my grandmothers.

A coworker who had passed from breast cancer.

My father.

Even my son, Nathaniel.

The things they said—the memories they brought up—were so personal, so clear, that I knew they couldn't have come from anyone else. These were people I loved—my family, my son. And somehow, they were all there, talking through him.

Some things aren't for the world to hear. And I'm okay keeping them that way. But there was one message they all seemed to agree on.

They saw my struggles. They saw the boundaries I was setting—with my mom, with myself, with the people around me.

And they were proud of me.

Then Bill paused. Closed his eyes for a moment, listening.

And said something I never expected.

"They're clapping for you."

I froze.

Clapping? Applauding?

I had spent months dealing with guilt—over saying no, over putting my needs first for once. I kept wondering if I was letting my mom down by putting distance between us. If I was giving up on her. If I was just being selfish.

And yet, here they were—my father, my son, the people I'd lost—cheering me on from beyond.

Not judging me. Not disappointed in me.

Proud.

Proud that I was learning to protect my own peace.

Proud that I was finally putting myself first.

Proud that, after years of taking care of everyone else, I was choosing me.

When the session ended, Bill hugged me again. Told me to stay on the path I was on. To keep healing. To keep setting boundaries.

And as I walked out of his office, I knew for sure:

I wasn't running from my well-being anymore.

I was finally running toward it.

Dear Red Straw

The thing about growing up with no boundaries is you don't even know they're missing—until you start trying to set them.

At first, it feels wrong. Like you're breaking some rule you didn't even know you were supposed to follow. Like you're turning your back on the people you've spent your whole life trying to look out for. You feel bad. You second-guess yourself. You hear that voice in your head asking if maybe you really are just being unfair.

But the only way to break free from all that is to step back—to finally put boundaries where there were none.

To stop feeling responsible for how other people feel.

To stop blaming yourself for things that weren't your fault.

To stop confusing love with giving yourself up.

Because love isn't about erasing yourself.

It's not about making yourself small so someone else can feel big.

It's not about saying yes until you fall apart.

Love needs boundaries. So do healthy relationships.

And setting them?

That's love too.

Jeremy Allen Damours

Dear Dad,

I don't think you meant to hurt us, but you did. Every time you reached back and smacked us in the head when we were irritating you in the car, it felt like you crossed a line. You didn't look like a strong man, but your hands were strong. Really strong.

So was the way your eyes looked when you hit us. Angry. Glassy. Like something was boiling under the surface. Your mouth would twist, your teeth would start gnashing. That's what scared me the most.

It always came out of nowhere. We'd be doing something—usually something we had no idea was bothering you—and then, smack. No warning. No chance to dodge it. We'd just sit there, stunned, trying to process what just happened. Trying to figure out what we did wrong.

Was it really about us being too loud? Or was it because you didn't want to be there, because we reminded you of what was

Dear Red Straw

keeping you from drinking? Was it because deep down, you knew you would always love Mom more than us? You told us that enough times growing up. Maybe it was all of it.

I could have let it go if it was just irritation. If it was just an overreaction. But your eyes. That's what stayed with me.

You always seemed happier at work than you did at home. And when you were home, you always found a way to be anywhere but with us.

But there were times we had you. And those are the moments I cherish. That day at the lake in northern Arizona. Watching the hot air balloons take off and eating donuts in Phoenix. Ice fishing on Birch Lake in Alaska. The few times we went to the state fair as a family.

Those times, it felt like we won. It was us, not the alcohol.

Chapter 7

Chasing The Reins

Letting her live with us changed everything.

We don't control others just to be controlling. It's because we're scared of what might happen. Of being hurt. Of feeling something we don't want to feel. So we try to stay in charge of everything, hoping it'll keep things from falling apart.

Living with someone you love who drinks makes you feel like you're losing control—over your day, the mood in the house, the alcohol showing up at your door, and whether they're about to hurt themselves—fall down the stairs, mix pills with alcohol, or do something dangerous without realizing it.

So you start doing whatever you can to hold things together.

You walk on eggshells. You study their mood—listening to their tone, watching their face, checking if they're angry, sad, or way too cheerful. You notice how they come into the room—if they're stumbling, if they're slurring, if their eyes are glazed over, or if something just feels off.

You smell them when they get close, trying to figure out if they've been drinking. You check the trash can outside for empty bottles—not because you don't already know they drink, but because they told you they stopped. Or they said they only had one, and now you're trying to make sense of their behavior—and how long they've been lying.

You do what you can to keep it from getting worse. You try to calm them down when they get upset. You clean up their messes—like spilled drinks or finding them half-dressed and stumbling around the house while your kids are home. You shut their bedroom door and tell them to stay put, then sit outside that door for hours, just to make sure they don't fall or wander out again.

You change the subject when certain things come up, like money, drinking, or anything that might make them feel like you're pointing a finger. All of it is just to keep things quiet for one more night.

I can see it now. I wasn't just trying to keep the peace—I was trying to stay in control. Not because I wanted power, but because I was scared. Scared of what might happen if I didn't stay two steps ahead. Scared of the damage. Scared of what my kids and Michael were seeing—and what it was doing to them. To us.

I thought if I could keep her moods in check, clean things up fast enough, keep things quiet enough—maybe I could stop everything from turning into a bigger mess.

We think we have control, but we don't. Not when their drinking comes first. We try to hold it together—but it wears us out. The stress, the anxiety, the pressure to stay ahead of whatever might go wrong—it builds up until there's nothing left. And then we break.

Jeremy Allen Damours

You don't notice the moment things fall apart. You just wake up inside the wreckage.

My mom was living with us, and her drinking was bad again. We were doing what we had to just to get through the days, hoping we'd figure out how to live with it. But it was getting harder to pretend things were okay.

She was lying about it—saying she wasn't drinking when I could tell she was. She even started going on dates with men who gave me a bad feeling. One said he was a geologist working on million-dollar deals overseas. Another drove in from another state just to take her out to dinner—then posted a photo on social media of himself and his meal, with her completely cropped out.

And they were always texting her asking for money.

I told her not to give out our address and asked her to meet them in public places instead. But they still showed up at the house, and when I asked her why, she said she forgot I told her not to share it.

She took everything the wrong way. If I didn't smile when I said "good morning," she thought I was mad—like she'd done something wrong and I was giving her the silent treatment. If I ran out to grab something from the store without saying goodbye, it wasn't just a quick trip in her mind—it meant I was upset and didn't want her to know where I was going. If I made myself dinner without telling her, she saw it as

Dear Red Straw

me leaving her out, like I had done it on purpose to hurt her. Every little thing became something bigger, something it wasn't.

It was her.

The way she was behaving wore me down. And the more worn down I got, the more it started spilling into how I treated everyone else. Instead of handling it better, I started doing the same things to Michael and the kids that she was doing to me.

If Michael seemed sad, I started to think it was my fault. If he didn't say something when I expected him to—like "good morning" right away—I figured I had done something wrong.

If my boys weren't talking to me as much as they normally did, I thought it was about me—even though I didn't used to take it that way. They were just being teenagers.

Feeling like I was losing control meant picking fights that didn't need to happen. It meant putting everyone on edge—wanting things from them that weren't fair. Like expecting Michael to read my mind, or expecting the boys to stay upbeat and go along with everything, no matter what. And the longer it went on, the more things fell apart.

We all stopped talking to each other and began doing more and more on our own.

Michael and I were avoiding each other—especially when my mom was around. And after a while, we were avoiding her too.

I began to wonder if something was wrong with me. That maybe I was being distant. Cold. But little by little, I started to see it for what it was. I wasn't the one making things uncomfortable. I wasn't the one turning normal moments into problems.

One morning, as I sat on the edge of the bed trying to wake up, I watched Michael get dressed for work. His face looked worn. His shoulders slumped. His eyes were blank, like there was nothing left in him. He stared down at the floor, lost in thought, and I couldn't help but wonder what was running through his head.

Was he thinking about us? About our family? About my mom? Maybe the life we were building together didn't make sense anymore. Was he remembering how it felt when we first met—how carefree it all used to be, before any of this? Was he regretting it all? Was he regretting me?

He could leave any moment. And if he did, I wouldn't blame him. This is not what he signed up for—it just got dropped on him. Sure, he said yes to letting my mom live with us, but he did it for me.

I thought about my boys—how unhappy they seemed. And how I was putting everything my parents put on me right onto them.

And that's when it sank in.

We were living my childhood—the one ruined by addiction.

"If I don't get her out of here, I'm going to ruin us even more," I blurted out, into the empty space between us.

Dear Red Straw

I looked at Michael and said it again.

He nodded.

And in that moment, I knew.

I couldn't control my mom.

I couldn't control my kids. I couldn't control Michael.

The only thing I could control was getting her out of our home—out of our lives.

Jeremy Allen Damours

My mom feared losing us—and her grip on control. So she used guilt. And now, I was doing the same thing.

From the start, before the fights and before my mom moved in, Michael was calm. Steady. Safe. And because I'd never had that before, it scared me. He was different, and I didn't want to lose him.

But I struggled with self-doubt. When we weren't together, I felt nervous, waiting to hear from him, wondering what he was doing, worrying about what it meant if he didn't call or reply to a text. I told myself I trusted him, and in my head, I did. But I still worried that if I wasn't around, if I wasn't part of what was happening, he might realize I wasn't enough. That my life, my kids, my past—everything I brought with me—would be too much for him.

One night, back when we were still dating, we went out to dinner with some of his friends. We stayed out—eating, drinking, laughing. It felt simple. Familiar. Like something I could actually picture lasting.

When it started getting late, we went back to my place so I could be there for the boys. I figured that was it for the night. I thought Michael would stay like he usually did.

But when we got home, he said he was going out to a nightclub with some different friends.

That's when the panic hit.

Dear Red Straw

As soon as he said those words, I felt it in my body. All the calm from earlier was gone. My mind flooded with questions.

Why are you going back out?

I thought you wanted to be here with me.

What are you planning to do?

I felt left out. Unwanted. Nervous—like something had changed, even though he hadn't done anything wrong.

I couldn't stop thinking about it. Was he bored with me? Did he regret coming back here first? Was he hoping to meet someone else? He didn't seem like the type to cheat—not really. But the thoughts were there.

After the panic came the loneliness. I loved my boys, but I felt trapped. I didn't have the same freedom Michael did. I couldn't just go out whenever I wanted—my life was wrapped around my kids. And as much as I loved them, I felt cut off. I wanted Michael to see that. I wanted him to stay—to understand how much I needed him.

"Don't go," I said, trying to keep my voice steady, but it came out shaky.

Then I said whatever I thought might make him stay. "I just thought you'd want to be here."

"Do you want to?"

It wasn't just about wanting him there. It was about needing to feel like I mattered.

Michael stared at the wall, jaw tight, arms crossed. His silence was saying everything.

I could feel it all—how annoyed he was, how tense it felt in the room, how much he probably wanted to say I was being out of line. That I was making him feel guilty when he hadn't done anything wrong. And he would've been right.

He didn't say anything for a long time. Just sat there, not looking at me.

When he finally spoke, his voice was quiet—almost like he didn't want to say it out loud.

"I told myself a long time ago," he said, "I'd never let a guy control me."

And the second I heard it, I knew—I was being that guy. The one he swore he'd never let in.

I thought he was going to walk out. Maybe he should've. But he didn't. He stayed. He chose me—at the cost of something he'd promised himself.

I tried to backpedal, told him he could still go—but it was too late. The damage was already done.

It took me years to really see what that night was about. It wasn't about trust. It wasn't about loyalty. It was about control. If he went out, I couldn't hold onto him. But if he stayed—if he was next to me—I could breathe. I could feel safe again. Like maybe I wasn't about to lose him.

Dear Red Straw

But control isn't always about the other person. Sometimes, it's about trying to be the version of ourselves we think they want.

Especially when that version is the only thing stopping them from seeing what they don't want to see.

My dad could change in an instant. A small comment, a look he didn't like, or an opinion he didn't agree with—that was all it took. One minute we'd be talking. The next, he'd turn it into an argument.

If I didn't let him have the final word, he'd get louder and repeat what he'd already said, over and over, like saying it again would make me back down. These didn't feel like real conversations. They weren't about understanding each other. They were about him being right. And if I didn't give in, things got worse.

But there were parts of me I didn't dare let him see. Things that didn't fit his idea of what a son was supposed to be. I didn't know what he'd do with that, and I didn't want to find out. So I started thinking ahead.

I was about thirteen, and we were all in the car together as a family, driving around town. It was an unusually clear winter day. The sun was so bright, its rays bounced off the snowbanks, and if you didn't look away fast enough, the glare would leave you blinking, temporarily blinded.

We were out running errands, like we usually did on the weekends. In a town that small, the same faces turned up everywhere. Most blended into the background without much thought. But there were a few that stood out every time.

They were the town's three gay hairdressers, and everyone knew who they were. In a place built on church, family, and tradition, they didn't just stand out—they challenged what people were used to. They dressed how they liked, acted how they felt, and didn't try to hide it for anyone. They didn't blend in, and they weren't trying to.

They all lived together and worked out of a small salon tucked inside one of the town's tiny, one-story malls.

Daddy was the leader—big, tough-looking, always serious, the one who seemed to be in charge. He was quiet and kind of intimidating. Kenny was the loud one—expressive, confident, full of energy. He was the one who brought most of the money in. Then there was Boy—soft-spoken like Daddy, kept to himself. You never really knew what he was thinking.

I remember Kenny once giving me a salacious look. I think he was just being playful—he wasn't afraid to show who he was.

Every time my dad saw them driving around together in their station wagon, he never missed a chance to say it.

"Hey, look! The Fagmobile!"

I laughed along because that's what I thought I was supposed to do. But it made me uneasy. I wasn't sure why at first. Maybe it was just how harsh his words

Dear Red Straw

were. Or maybe, deep down, I already knew I was hiding something.

My laugh felt fake, and the pit in my stomach twisted tighter the more I thought about it. I knew "fag" was a bad word—even though my dad said it like a joke, like it was just something funny to say when they drove by. And if that word was about them, what did that mean for me? I'd already started noticing things—feelings I didn't know what to do with. It felt like whatever I was becoming must've been wrong.

My dad didn't know I was gay. And now, I wasn't about to let him find out.

If he could get upset over something small—like a look, a joke, or a comment he didn't agree with—what would he do with the truth about me?

I started being more careful, making sure I wouldn't catch his attention in the wrong way. One of the things I did was cover my bedroom walls with supermodel posters. Cindy Crawford was everywhere back then, and I hung up three or four big ones of her in a bikini—right where he'd see them.

The first time my dad saw them, he grinned—glass in hand, ice clinking against the sides, his skinny red straw bobbing with each movement. His eyes lit up, like the sight of Cindy's body snapped him out of his drunken state for just a few seconds. Then he nodded, almost to himself, and muttered, "That's my boy."

The performance had worked.

I had made sure he saw what I wanted him to.

And still, I felt like a complete fraud.

Jeremy Allen Damours

I was busy hiding one truth while their marriage was breaking in front of me.

Aside from being found out, the idea of my parents splitting up was one of the things that scared me the most. It just didn't seem possible.

The fighting, the drinking, the chaos—it was taking a toll on us. Not always in big, obvious ways. It was slow. Quiet. And by the time we were old enough to leave home, the damage had already settled in.

We didn't feel that damage right away, though. Not until we got jobs, started dating, and tried to figure out who we were outside of the house. That's when things got harder. We struggled with stress, had trouble trusting people, didn't really know who we were.

But while we were growing up and starting to deal with all that, nothing changed at home.

They kept drinking and acting like it wasn't a problem. And each one made it easier for the other not to stop.

Later, I'd realize that if one of them ever did stop, it wouldn't work between them anymore.

But the drinking didn't stop. It kept going—years of it. And the longer it went on, the more we paid for it too.

One morning, when I was fourteen, I was in the car with my parents on the way to town for groceries.

Dear Red Straw

They had been arguing about money since we left the house.

About halfway there, they started yelling at each other.

"Why do you always do that, Kathy? I hate it when you do that!"

"What do you mean, 'Why do I always do that,' Danny? They needed new coats and gloves and shoes for winter—they just can't go without!"

"Goddammit, Kathy! You know we don't have the money right now! I hate it when you spend money without asking me. Goddammit to hell!"

"I could just... I could just..."

"What? You could just do what to me right now?"

"You know better than to spend money without asking first! We don't have the money right now!"

"Do you want to get a divorce? Maybe we just need to get a divorce!"

Divorce? Where did that come from?

I'd never heard my mom use that word before. If she said it, she had to be really angry. My dad sounded like he was about to lose it—but that was normal. What caught me off guard was hearing it from her. I froze. My heart was racing. I didn't know what to do with the feeling.

I started imagining what it would be like if they actually got divorced. Our home, split in two. Everything familiar—gone overnight. Could this car ride be the start of them drifting apart? Where would the love in our house go? How could life ever feel normal again?

I thought about one of my friends whose parents were divorced—how he spent one week with his mom and the next with his dad. I imagined visiting my dad's place, how quiet it would be, how empty it would feel without my mom.

Then I pictured my mom's place—brighter, warmer, more talking, more love. But no matter how hard I tried, I couldn't see her alone in her own space. It felt unreal. Impossible. Would I have two bedrooms? Two houses? Two lives?

It was too much.

Their yelling got louder—so loud it started to hurt my ears.

I couldn't take it anymore.

"Stop yelling at each other and start acting like adults!"

Silence.

They sat there, quiet. Like my words had stunned them. I had called them out. Told them to act like adults. They didn't expect it.

I wondered if I'd gone too far—if they were going to snap at me for it.

But they didn't.

None of us said a word for the rest of the ride into town.

Dear Red Straw

And I didn't get in trouble for telling the adults to act like adults.

They didn't split up.

But something in me did.

I was just a kid trying to keep it from getting worse.

Jeremy Allen Damours

Control feels like safety. Like stability. Like the only way to keep life from falling apart. But it doesn't always fix what's underneath it.

For a long time, I thought if I just kept things together—if I made sure my dad saw me the way he wanted, if I didn't let my mom's drinking mess up the house too much after he was gone, if I kept people close but not too close—then maybe nothing would fall apart. But the truth is, I wasn't really holding anything together. I was just scared.

Scared of losing people.

Scared of being vulnerable.

Scared of what to do with emotions I didn't know how to process.

And that fear made me try to control everything, thinking it would keep me safe. Thinking it would keep the people I loved safe.

But control doesn't keep us safe. It doesn't fix anything. It doesn't stop the past from creeping into the present. It just keeps us stuck, trying to manage everything, thinking that means we're okay.

Letting go doesn't mean giving up. It doesn't mean accepting chaos. It means recognizing where our responsibility ends and where life has to take its own course. Sometimes, the things we try hardest to control are the very things that need to be seen for what they are—not controlled.

Dear Red Straw

When we stop wasting energy trying to manage things that were never ours to control, we free ourselves to focus on what truly matters: our own happiness, our growth, our relationships, and the life we want to build. Because the things beyond our control will unfold with or without us—but the way we shape ourselves is entirely up to us.

Because real stability doesn't come from trying to control people—it comes from learning to sit with ourselves, to face our fears instead of putting them on others, to stop trying to stay in charge of everything and start trusting that we can handle life, even when we're not the ones in control.

Jeremy Allen Damours

Dear Mom,

I was excited when you called me, asking if the boys could come stay with you for the summer. You had just left Dad, and I was hoping it was for good this time. You were settling into your new place in Arizona, and even though it wasn't the first time I let myself believe you were changing for the better, this time felt different. Maybe because you had finally gotten the nerve to leave him. Maybe because I wanted so badly to believe it. Either way, I convinced myself this might actually be your turning point. That maybe you were serious.

Thinking back on that phone call now, I can't believe how naive I was. Naive for still underestimating just how deep your alcoholism ran. Stupid for thinking you could handle watching the boys on your own, day in and day out, with no help. Especially after all the times in the past when you'd beg me to let them stay the night with you and Dad, only to call me a few hours later, overwhelmed, asking me to come pick them

Dear Red Straw

up. I should have known better. I should have known not to put the boys in the middle of your alcoholism—the same way you put me in the middle of it. I should have known not to put myself back in it again, like I've done time and time before.

I guess part of me wanted to believe that now that Dad was out of the picture, maybe you'd finally get your shit together. But I should have known better. You weren't serious about leaving him. You weren't serious about quitting drinking. You weren't serious about anything. Deep down, I probably knew it was only a matter of time before you caved and went back to him.

What angers me most is how much control you had over all of us. Over me. Over my brothers. Over everyone in the family. You were so good at lying, so good at building a facade, making us believe every word you said. When you needed money for alcohol, you'd tell us it was for a utility bill, groceries, a prescription copay, a threatening bill collector. You had an excuse for everything. And we'd believe you. Like idiots, we'd believe you. Every single time.

Jeremy Allen Damours

Even when we confronted you, asking if you were drinking—you'd lie. Always. Even when the lies were so stupid, they were almost laughable. Like the time you said you were going to a new friend's house to bake cookies. Mom, you never baked cookies after we were grown. And yet somehow, every other day, you were back over there "baking cookies" again. It didn't take long before I realized those visits weren't really about cookies.

I still let myself hope. I wanted to believe you.

I took time off work, unpaid time off by the way, packed the boys into the car, and drove sixteen hours straight to Arizona. Sixteen hours. Because I wanted you to have that summer with them. Because I wanted them to have that summer with you.

And by the way, we almost died getting there.

I never told you that part.

We were driving through New Mexico. The sky was clear and blue — it was beautiful. Then, out of nowhere, dark clouds began chasing away the sun. At first, it was just a light sprinkle. I remember the rain falling, sparkling in the sunlight like tiny diamonds dropping from the sky. And then, without warning, the sun disappeared and the rain turned violent.

The rain became so thick that I could no longer see out of my windshield. Water rushed along the sides of the road, turning the long, lonely highway into a gushing river. I felt the tires losing grip. The car was sliding. The boys were dead silent, but I could see the fear in their eyes—they could tell we were in danger and it was too late for me to do anything about it.

I looked out the window, scanning for poles, trees, anything to grab onto if we had to abandon the car and fight against the current. Then, another thought hit me like a gut punch: What about the other cars? The semi-trucks? If one came up behind us too fast, unable to see us through the wall of rain, we'd be dead.

And all because I was dumb enough to bring them to you, thinking it would somehow be different this time. Just as I was beginning to panic even more, the rain finally stopped. We weren't swept away. We made it through. I was so relieved.

And when we finally got to Arizona, I should have turned right around and driven the boys back home.

I should have known the second I pulled into town and found you at the bar, finishing your drink.

I should have known.

But I didn't.

Because your control over me was so deep.

A couple of days later, I headed back to Texas, alone. It was a lonely sixteen-hour drive back, but I kept telling myself the boys were safe with you.

When I finally got back home, all I wanted was to collapse on the couch and sleep. I was excited for the time alone. I was excited for the boys to have a summer with their

Dear Red Straw

grandmother—a summer they'd remember, a summer they'd hopefully talk about for years.

So when Aunt Terry called me, furious, just fifteen minutes after I got home, I couldn't believe it.

She tore into me, angry that I had dumped the boys on you. Angry that I had left so soon without spending more time in Arizona. She was so angry, she told me that I was being a bad father.

I was stunned. I didn't know what she was talking about. I didn't understand where her anger was coming from. YOU had asked me to bring them. YOU wanted this.

YOU must have told her a different story. One that wasn't true.

You probably told her I just dropped them off and left.

You probably told her you couldn't handle them for the whole summer.

You probably told her you needed me to come back and get them.

Mom, I had only been gone for half a day! I had just driven 800 miles back home.

You couldn't even last a day before changing the story. Before twisting it. Before making me the villain, making me the irresponsible one, making me the bad father.

You had no respect for my time.

You had no respect for my reputation.

You had no respect for the boys.

I'll never fully understand why you asked for them that summer, knowing you couldn't handle it. Knowing you weren't ready. Knowing you had no intention of following through.

All I know is that you were a master manipulator.

A master controller.

You had control over me then.

But I swear you'll never control me like that again.

CHAPTER 8

TANGLED TIES

Some of the hardest problems to fix are the ones we didn't even know were there. The way things were in our families growing up stuck with us more than we knew. What we learned as kids still affects how we get close to people now, whether we're dating them or just trying to be friends.

Some of us made it out of our homes relatively untouched. But most of us didn't. We were changed in ways that didn't fully show until later. And by the time we start to understand just how much damage was done, years—sometimes decades—have already passed.

We don't always see how much our messy childhoods still get in the way of how we connect to people now. Being around all that drama and tension growing up left a lot of us with attachment issues, fear of being left, and a shaky sense of self-worth.

We got used to trying to get people to like us— just to feel seen, important, or even just okay. Since we didn't grow up with clear lines around what was okay and what wasn't, it became hard to draw those lines later. So we leaned too much on other people to feel better.

But people can't hold all that for us. They've got their own stuff, their own limits. And sooner or later, they let us down—not because they're bad, but because they're human.

There was a time in our lives when someone showed us how to tie our shoes. They did it first, then handed us the laces and told us to try. We messed it up over and over—sometimes getting knots, sometimes not even getting that far before we had to start all over again.

But after a while, we got it. Figuring out how to tie the laces wasn't so confusing anymore. Eventually, we could do it without even thinking. We even showed other people how to do it, too.

When you find yourself caught in a mess as an adult, think back to when you were learning to tie your shoes. First, you crossed the laces, made a loop, wrapped the other lace around, and pulled it through—sometimes messing it up completely. You'd start over, fumble again, then finally get it. And once you got it, you never forgot.

If you mess up along the way, pause and think about why. Did you say or do something too fast without knowing the whole story? Did your lack of trust make you assume the worst?

Are you not giving them enough space? Are you doing things that make them uncomfortable—or that make you uncomfortable?

Are your fears or doubts getting in the way—making it hard to talk or stopping you from doing anything at all? Are things falling apart because no one's really talking?

There are a lot of reasons things go wrong. Sometimes, we just need to look at it for what it is.

Jeremy Allen Damours

Some knots don't come undone right away. I had to fumble through a few the hard way.

I don't remember a time in my childhood when my parents did things separately. They were always together—waking up at the same time, eating at the same time, hitting the bottle at the same time.

They'd even leave for work at the same time. My dad planned his whole day around my mom's more rigid schedule—just another excuse for why she didn't need a driver's license.

If a coworker offered to drive her home when she had to stay late, or a friend asked her to lunch, he'd get irritated. It was like everything had to go through him.

So not surprisingly, I grew up thinking that being close meant doing everything together. I'd get upset when someone I cared about did something without me—like they were mad or didn't want me around.

It didn't occur to me that maybe they just needed space—or just wanted time with other people.

I didn't realize how much I depended on others to feel wanted and safe—because that's what I saw growing up.

I can see now how much I lost myself trying to hold on to people. I was clinging to them. I needed to feel like I mattered.

Dear Red Straw

If any relationship showed me how lost I could get in someone else, it was the one I had with Roderick.

I was in my early twenties, fresh off a divorce and newly moved to Texas, when I met Roderick. This was before I met Michael. I liked him right away. He was tall and lean, with mocha brown skin and a chiseled jawline. There was something about him—just a little edge—that made him interesting. And underneath that edge, there was this calm way he had with my two boys, who were toddlers at the time. That felt rare. And I was starving for something that felt real.

At first, he made me feel like I mattered. He texted me all the time, asking when I could come over. He'd ask what I felt like eating, where I wanted to go. When he came to my place, he never said a word about what he didn't like. He never made me feel like there was anything wrong with me—or how I lived.

After a few months of dating—and spending almost every day together—Roderick asked if we should move in. I hesitated. Deep down, I knew it was too soon. I knew it wasn't a good idea. But I didn't want to lose him, so I ignored that feeling and said yes. We found a two-bedroom apartment and moved in. I told myself it would work out.

But things changed as soon as we got the keys.

On move-in day, Roderick suddenly acted like the place was his. He chose what furniture we'd keep—his—and what we'd get rid of—mine. My things were trashed or shoved into storage. He picked the decorations, set things up how he wanted, and made all the decisions about where everything should go. I wasn't asked. When I tried to say something—quietly suggesting something I wanted—he acted like it was stupid and gave me some excuse about why his way was better.

By the time everything was in place, it didn't feel like our home. It felt like his. But I didn't say anything. I was too scared to cause a problem. I didn't want to upset him or give him a reason to leave. So I let it all go—what I liked, what I thought, what I needed.

And that was just the beginning.

We started arguing more. He never yelled or hit me. He never said it had to be his way. But he had this quiet way of deciding how things would go—by brushing off my opinions, by making me feel like speaking up was silly or selfish. And because I was scared to disagree, he always got his way. He knew the parts of me that were unsure, and he used them.

Then he just let it show.

Roderick started inviting people over late at night without asking me. I'd be in bed by 1 or 2 a.m., and he'd show up with a group of friends from the club—loud and laughing—ignoring the fact that the boys were asleep and I had work in the morning. He treated our home like a party pad, not a place where two small kids were trying to grow up.

I think he realized that living with kids meant doing more—not just saying the right things, but actually being there. I was trying to bring routine into our lives and keep things calm and stable. But maybe that made him feel boxed in. Maybe he felt guilty. Or maybe he saw the boys as getting in the way of the

Dear Red Straw

freedom he wanted—the late nights, the parties, the last-minute plans.

And he didn't stop.

One night, I was lying in bed, wide awake. Roderick still wasn't home. I didn't know where he was, but I was used to that by then. I kept telling myself not to make a big deal out of it. He'd probably just gone out for drinks with the guys. I stayed up, waiting for him.

Sometime around 2 a.m., I heard the front door open. Then came laughter—loud, sloppy, drunk. He hadn't come home alone. I could hear him and a group of friends in the dining room, talking over each other, making noise like they didn't care what time it was. My boys were asleep down the hall. I had to be up in a few hours. But none of that seemed to matter to him.

I laid there, staring at the ceiling, hoping they'd quiet down soon. But something didn't feel right. The sound of their voices changed. Less laughing. More whispering.

Then silence.

I knew something was off, so I got up and crept to the door, cracking it open. There was Roderick—kissing one of his friends like I wasn't on the other side seeing it.

I just stood there, watching. Thinking. I was the one who had rearranged my whole life to be here. And for what? This?

I felt betrayed. Sad. Empty. And a quiet knowing this wasn't going to work. No matter how much I tried. No matter how much I gave.

Jeremy Allen Damours

I had spent the last six months clinging to who I hoped he could be. Even if it meant me having to stop being myself along the way. Or was I ever myself at all?

We fought after that night. I told him I'd had enough—I was done. But he didn't argue. He didn't beg me to stay. He barely reacted at all. Just cold. Distant. Like none of it meant anything.

A couple nights later, I went back to grab the last of my things. His same friends from that night were there, and when they let me in, I walked straight into Roderick all over another guy.

He knew I was standing there. He didn't stop. Didn't say a word. Didn't even look at me.

And somehow, that moment—his complete indifference—just confirmed what I already knew. I had lost myself trying to keep someone who was never really there.

Dear Red Straw

After Roderick, I started noticing it in other parts of my life. How much of my energy went into being what other people needed—like that was the only way I'd ever be worth loving.

I've always felt a quiet frustration with myself for that. For tying my worth to how others were doing. Making sure they were okay. That they weren't hurting. That they were happy. That they felt seen and cared for.

It's like I have to help—and if I can't, I feel guilty. Guilty when I try and fail. Guilty when I'm not enough. Guilty when someone I care about is still in pain, even though they don't know I'm feeling it too, wishing I could take it away.

Sometimes I envy people who aren't like that. People who don't take on so much. Who don't feel the need to fix everything. I wonder what it's like to just think about yourself. To not get pulled into everyone else's problems all the time.

Still, that same thing that wears me out is also what lifts me up—especially when it leads to something good.

I feel almost high when I'm able to help someone. Like I did what I was meant to do. Like I solved something, eased someone's struggle, got them through it. And now they get to keep going—because of me. It gives me a sense of worth. A reason to get up. A reason to exist.

But it's not always that simple. Sometimes you walk away and wonder if you messed up.

One day, I was just about to walk into the grocery store when I saw a woman coming toward me. She wasn't in a rush, but it was clear she wanted something. Right before I reached the sliding doors, she stepped in front of me. Not aggressively. Just enough so I couldn't pretend not to see her. So I stopped.

She looked tired—not just her body, but her face too. Her eyes said she hadn't rested in a long time. Her mouth was stiff, like she was doing everything she could not to cry. Life had been hard on her for a while. Two little boys stood beside her, staying close and not saying a word.

She started pleading softly, said she was down on her luck and needed money to take care of her sons. She didn't seem homeless—just like someone who needed a hand.

I didn't know what to say at first. I froze for a second, then gave her a quiet "sorry" and kept walking. She stepped aside, looked at her boys, and didn't say a word.

But she stayed in my head.

It's weird when stuff like that catches you off guard. Sometimes things are going okay, and it's easy to give—money, food, a kind word. But other times, you're just trying to get by yourself.

That was one of those times for me.

I was between jobs, trying to save every dollar. I didn't feel like I could spare any money, even though

Dear Red Straw

I wanted to help. And I wasn't even sure if I could trust her. People lie. People take advantage. And I didn't want to be a fool.

But as I walked through the store, it hung over me. Her and the two boys. I kept thinking maybe she really was going through something rough and needed help.

I remembered a time when someone helped us. One Thanksgiving, when my parents had no money, a group of people from the bank my mom worked at left bags of food on our doorstep. No knock, no names—just kindness. I remember my mom crying when she opened the door.

And even though I didn't have much in my bank account, I could still do something small.

I stood there, hating how it felt. I couldn't leave her like that.

I went back through the aisles, grabbing a rotisserie chicken, two chocolate milks for the boys, and a bottle of water for her. As I stood in line to pay, I felt a little spark—like maybe this small gesture could make their night a little easier.

But when I got outside, they were nowhere.

I searched the parking lot. Drove around the area. I couldn't find them. The longer I looked, the worse I felt. Not because I had said no at first, but because I didn't get to make it right. I started blaming myself for taking too long. For not acting fast enough. For not being the person I should've been in that moment.

I never saw her again—and that still bothers me.

I felt torn. Like helping meant I had to say yes, no matter what—and saying no made me feel like I was letting her down.

Not because I did something wrong. Not because I didn't care. But because moments like that still get tangled up with how I was raised. I grew up thinking I had to say yes. That I had to fix things. That if I didn't, it meant something was wrong with me.

But it doesn't.

It was okay to say no that day. I was trying to take care of myself. And even when I changed my mind, it was still okay. I didn't fail just because I couldn't fix it.

This is what untangling is—learning to help without guilt. Caring without taking on more than you can handle. Giving yourself permission to walk away sometimes, and still believing you're a good person.

Dear Red Straw

Before Roderick. Before the woman at the grocery store. Before I ever started questioning why I felt responsible for everyone else's pain—there was Yvette.

It didn't start with fireworks. Just nervous energy, school lunches, and a quiet feeling that this girl really saw me.

I was a sophomore in high school and friends with her cousin, Marie—a sweet, shy Alaska Native girl, tall and wiry, with a long black ponytail and glowing brown skin. None of us would've guessed she'd grow up to be a Marine.

Like me, she was a little nerdy—just more outgoing. But she never made me feel weird for being quiet. She was down-to-earth, easy to be around, and nice to everyone. Just the kind of person you wanted to be friends with.

I could be my quiet, awkward self all day, and she never made a big deal about it. She had a way of getting me to talk, and gently pushing me to speak up more around the other kids.

We had a routine of eating lunch together every day under one of the school's main stairwells. Lunch started at 10:50 a.m.—a weird time, but the school had to split everyone into three lunch periods, and we got stuck with the early one.

For a couple months, it was just the two of us—until the day Marie brought Yvette around.

Jeremy Allen Damours

I still remember the moment I first noticed Yvette. Her face had the soft shape of a heart, tapering at the chin and curving into her neck like it belonged there. There was a warm ivory glow to her skin, like sunlight brushed across brown clay. And her eyes—gently curved, with whites so soft they made you pause held something calm and open, like they were letting you in without trying to.

She had a laugh that was loud but gentle, like happiness that didn't need to ask for permission. It was tender. Like she was simply glad to be in the moment.

A few weeks after Yvette started having lunch with us, Marie looked over at me and said, "She likes you, you know." Just like that. No warning. No reason. Just said it out of nowhere.

It was the first time I ever knew for sure that a girl liked me.

And I was nervous. I'd liked girls before, but none of them had ever liked me back. Most of them were confusing.

There was one girl, Jessica, that same year who hated me for reasons I could never figure out. I hated her too, mostly because she hated me. One day in art class, she yanked my hair just to be mean. I was so mad I stood up, yanked her hair back, and told her if she ever did that again, I'd beat her up.

Of course, I wasn't serious.

She was stunned—definitely didn't expect me to stand up for myself. I kind of stunned myself too. It just happened, like a reflex, after years of her insults.

Dear Red Straw

She never bothered me again after that.

Yvette wasn't anything like her. But I still had no idea what to do with that kind of attention.

I didn't mean to back off—I just didn't know what to do with someone wanting to be close to me. But I pulled away anyway. And still, Yvette stuck around. Laughing at my jokes. Sitting near me. Finding little ways to stay close.

Then one day, she stopped.

And that's when I noticed it—like something was missing. Like I'd pushed her away and didn't realize what I had until it wasn't there anymore.

At first, I didn't know what to do. I just knew I missed her. I didn't like how it felt with her gone.

So I went after her.

We were only sixteen. But we started spending more time together. Talking more. Hanging out at each other's houses. Lying around, watching TV. Laughing at dumb stuff.

There wasn't some big moment where it all changed—it just happened. It felt easy being around her. And little by little, it started to feel like love.

And with that love, at seventeen, our son Nathaniel was born.

But Nathaniel had a rare genetic disease. And a year after he came into our lives, he was gone.

He became the center of our love. The glue that held us together when things got hard. In a way, he made us feel complete.

Jeremy Allen Damours

When he died, that feeling we had, like things made sense, went with him. So did the comfort we found in each other.

After that, I tried to hold it together the best I could.

As the years passed, I gave nearly everything I had. I worked full-time and told her she didn't need to work as long as we had enough to get by. I just wanted her to feel safe. Cared for.

When her aunt needed a place to stay, I didn't complain. We just made room.

And when her mom came around to sober up—like the time she got so drunk she tripped and fell through our old living room window—I stayed calm, even when the glass shattered everywhere. Those antique shards could've seriously hurt her. Could've killed her.

But things kept getting harder—especially after I finished nursing school.

By then, we had Levi. He didn't have the disease that took Nathaniel. But parenting was hard on Yvette. She didn't seem happy anymore. Something in her changed after Nathaniel died, and it never really came back.

She started being gone more. Sometimes for hours. Sometimes all night. And I stayed home with Levi, feeling more alone than ever.

We were just kids, trying to act like adults—trying to build a life when we had no idea what we were doing. I didn't speak up much. I let her do what she

Dear Red Straw

wanted because I didn't want to argue. If she spent money we didn't have, I kept quiet. If something felt unfair, I just held it in.

Little by little, that became our normal. We didn't talk about what wasn't working. We didn't talk about how we felt. If something bothered one of us, we let it sit. If something needed to be said, we avoided it.

We didn't fall apart in some big dramatic way. It just faded—slowly—until we were living in the same house but not really in the same relationship anymore.

And after we had Devin, raising two kids became too much for her. She just wasn't ready. She wasn't in a place where she could handle it. And maybe she knew that before I did. What she needed most was space to breathe—and in the end, that's what she took.

It wasn't just me getting caught in the moment anymore. It was me building a whole life around keeping things together—and forgetting there was a "me" in it at all.

Jeremy Allen Damours

Yvette was the first. But I was still stuck in the only version of love I knew—one built on fear, silence, and holding it all in.

Roderick came after. Then Dido. And eventually, Michael.

They were early mistakes—me trying to love with a broken idea of what love even was.

Hard lessons I didn't see coming.

Dido was young and full of big dreams—but he didn't have a way to make them happen. He worked at a restaurant and was taking some college classes, but they didn't seem to be leading anywhere. And even though he was great at tennis, he wasn't quite good enough to make it into the big leagues. He was stuck—drifting, not sure what came next.

Though things between us seemed good, we weren't on the same path.

I had a full-time job, bills to pay, and daycare wasn't cheap. I was living on my own, handling what life kept throwing at me. He was still living at home, surrounded by family, with nothing pushing him to grow up. I needed something that wouldn't fall apart—something I could count on. He just wanted to be free, away from anything that felt like pressure.

So he started to pull away—slowly, quietly. He stopped inviting me over. Took longer to reply to my messages. Didn't seem as eager to spend time with me. I could feel it, even before I had proof.

Dear Red Straw

When he finally admitted he couldn't handle being around my kids—even though I never asked him to take care of them—he didn't really know how to end things with me. I could tell he had already checked out long before he said the words. He just didn't have it in him to say them out loud. And deep down, I knew I'd have to be the one to give him permission to let go of us.

One night, I sat down and wrote him a letter. I told him what I was seeing. Asked if he still wanted to be with me. Told him it was okay if he didn't. That if his heart wasn't in it anymore, he didn't have to pretend.

I wasn't angry. I just needed to know.

That's when he came over. He sat on the edge of my bed and told me I was right. I didn't cry. I just nodded. Like I already knew.

And when it came time to say goodbye, he wouldn't hug me. Not because he was upset or trying to be distant—but because he didn't want to confuse things. He said touching me might make it feel like things weren't really over. That the kindest thing he could do was walk away.

So he did. And that was the end of us.

The next few weeks were rough. I fell into a deep depression. I kept checking my phone, staring out the window, reloading social media—hoping he'd change his mind and come back to me. But he never did. I started to question if I'd made it too easy for him to go.

Jeremy Allen Damours

So there I was—looking back at a bunch of relationships that didn't work. It felt like I kept choosing the wrong people—people who didn't really love me, didn't treat me right, or didn't have the patience to meet me where I was. Maybe it was all of the above.

I wasn't sure I had it in me to try again. But I did.

By the time I met Michael, I honestly thought I'd never figure it out. I was still holding onto a lot of old stuff—still stuck on to a broken idea of how love was supposed to work.

So I left some things out. When we first met, I didn't even tell him I had kids. I was scared he'd leave me like Dido did.

He found out a few weeks later, when I had to cancel on him one night because I didn't have a sitter. He didn't run. He just listened.

I kept other things to myself, too—like how I couldn't keep a job for long. Sometimes I got bored and wanted something different. Other times, someone at work upset me or something big changed, and I'd panic and quit.

I jumped between part-time jobs in home care—places where everything felt messy. People didn't talk to each other. The ones in charge didn't know what they were doing. Just stressful all around. I'd stay until it got to be too much, and then I'd leave.

I never told him before I quit. I didn't want to see the concern in his face or hear the truth I wasn't ready for.

Dear Red Straw

I was scared. I didn't want him to be mad. I didn't want to seem like someone he couldn't count on. I thought if I could find a new job before he noticed, maybe he wouldn't have a reason to leave me.

But he did catch on. And he was never angry.

Instead, he reminded me—gently—that I deserved to find a job I liked. One I could grow in. A place I could stay at for a while without it falling apart.

I didn't want to hear it. Because it made me feel like I'd already failed.

I kept everything inside. Like I'd always done. I was scared to say how I really felt—scared of how he might react, even though he'd never given me a reason to be afraid. I didn't know how to just be real with someone. I thought I had to act like I had it all together—even though deep down, I knew he could already see I didn't.

I was still doing the same things I'd learned to do growing up around alcohol—shutting down, hiding, trying to avoid conflict. And those habits would've continued to ruin my life—if Michael hadn't been who he was.

Even now, Michael helps untangle all of it—not by fixing me, but by staying. He gives me space to loosen the knots myself. He's my mirror. And when I look at him, I see myself—completely real, nothing hidden.

He lets me fall. And lets me get back up.

If love had a shape, his would be solid. Quiet. Unshakable.

Jeremy Allen Damours

What makes these kinds of ties so hard to see is how familiar they feel. We don't always see them as unhealthy, because they're all we've ever known. They show up in the quiet guilt we carry. In the way we say sorry for needing something. In the panic we feel when someone starts to drift away. We twist ourselves to avoid tension. We do too much to feel useful. We stay quiet so we don't cause problems.

Sometimes we think we've moved on from the past, but then it shows up in a relationship where we give too much, or in a moment when we realize we don't even know what we need—only what everyone else needs from us.

But there's something powerful in seeing these knots for what they are.

We don't have to keep doing the same things over and over. We don't have to keep tying ourselves to people who can't meet us halfway. And we don't have to stay wrapped in guilt, thinking it's love.

Letting go of what was passed down isn't about blame. It's about choosing something better now. It's about trusting that we're allowed to take up space in our own lives. That love doesn't have to cost us our voice. That we can be kind and still have boundaries. That we can be there for people without losing ourselves.

The healing takes time—one realization, one untied knot at a time.

Dear Red Straw

And with each knot we loosen, we make more room to become who we were always meant to be.

Jeremy Allen Damours

Dear Mom and Dad,

My gut told me it wasn't a good idea for us to live together again. I figured maybe it was because you were worried about not being able to afford rent on your own.

I know you both liked being around Devin and Levi— but only in small bursts. And if I'm being honest, it never really felt like moving in together was about wanting to be closer to me or the boys. It felt more like a way to save money so you could keep drinking comfortably without worrying about running out of money on rent.

I was a fool. I don't know why I let myself think it would be different this time. How did I ever convince myself we'd be happy with this arrangement? I must have forgotten what it was like growing up. I think I suppressed just how dysfunctional things had been.

Dad, when I got that new job after being out of work, you told me you wanted to watch the boys while I worked so I could save

Dear Red Straw

money on daycare. I didn't ask you—you offered. You said you could handle it. You swore you could.

I couldn't believe it when Mom called just a few hours after I got to work to say that you told her you couldn't handle watching them. You didn't even call me yourself.

Why?

Why did you say yes if you didn't mean it?

That was my third day at a brand-new job. My boss was already being difficult, and I could tell the job wasn't going to be a good fit. But I needed the money. And asking to go home early because you bailed on watching your grandkids—I knew that wasn't going to go well. It didn't. And eventually, that was just another reason I got fired altogether.

All because you wanted to dump your priorities to drink.

Seagram's 7 Crown and 7-Up. The skinny red straw. Sucking like it was the highlight of your day. Like nothing else mattered. You'd drink from it like it was something really special. Like you worshipped it. I could see it written on your face. The way your eyes got glassy as the day went on, the way you slowly checked out. It felt like you loved your addiction more than being with us.

  I didn't want to say anything in front of the boys. They were still so little. I didn't want them to see me angry. I just got quiet. I felt physically sick. My stomach was in knots. I was scared about getting fired, scared about money, and worst of all, I felt like I couldn't trust you anymore.

  And then, like that wasn't enough, you canceled my car insurance without telling me.

  You let me drive around for a week with no coverage. And you knew I was driving. You knew I had the boys in the car. You knew what kind of danger that put us in.

  Why didn't you just man up and tell me the cost of insurance was too high? I was paying you my share. All you had to do was

Dear Red Straw

tell me the truth. Instead, you just cancelled it without giving me a chance to find my own coverage. I only found out because I randomly asked if you had made the payment.

That hurt. Really bad.

It felt like deception.

Parents aren't supposed to do that to their children. Where was the concern? The care? The love? The respect?

The truth is, I struggled more once we moved in together. I should've never let it happen. I should've protected myself and the boys. But I didn't. I let you back into my life, and you brought the same alcoholic dysfunction with you. You tried to wrap me back into it—just like when I was a kid.

And shame on me, I let you.

CHAPTER 9

THE WEIGHT OF RELAPSE

Before my mom's first relapse, I used to think going back to drinking meant failure. She tried. She slipped. End of story.

I didn't understand that relapse is something many alcoholics go through. It happens—usually more than once. That doesn't mean they're hopeless or weak. It just means the road is hard.

And I'm not trying to make excuses. I say that with love and honesty.

I've seen it happen. One day she's doing okay. The next, something throws her off. A bad mood. An argument. Too much time alone. And just like that, she starts drinking again.

I've learned not to see it as the end. It's just part of what happens.

What matters more to me now is what she learns each time. Whether she remembers what went wrong. Whether she understands what triggered it. Whether she makes different choices the next time things get hard.

That's what I look for now. And even with all that, I still hope she finds a way to stay sober. Not just for a week or a month—but for real.

But I'm not naive. I know that staying off alcohol means paying attention—every single day. To your thoughts. The people around you. The places you go. And the things that influence you. Stress, triggers, emotions—all of it. Any one of those can pull you back in.

I've also come to see that alcohol is one of the hardest habits to quit. It's sneaky, always around, and easy to grab. And the world doesn't make it any easier. No one's taking the bottles off the shelves. No one's stopping you at the register. You're on your own.

But alcoholics are people—just like anyone else. They have their own pain, their own struggles. I try to keep that in mind. It helps me understand them.

But that doesn't mean everything they do is okay. It doesn't make it right when their drinking causes harm. And it doesn't make the drinking okay. But it does help me see the bigger picture.

It's how I've been able to keep some kindness in my heart—and not lose myself in all of it. It's the only way I've been able to make peace with the things I went through growing up.

If we really want to understand the people we love who are dealing with addiction—and if we want to understand ourselves—we have to look at everything. Not just the moments when they mess up, but what led to it. The habits. The pain. And the effort it takes just to try again.

Dear Red Straw

Sometimes, it takes a major loss to wake something up inside you. For my mom, that turning point came when my dad's body started breaking down—after decades of drinking. His health didn't get worse quickly, and it didn't happen quietly. Watching it fall apart day by day changed everything.

My parents' marriage ended nearly forty years after it began when my dad died just before his sixty-first birthday. The cause was brain damage from years of alcohol use—frontotemporal dementia.

Watching him get worse changed more than just how my mom saw him. It changed how she saw herself. It might've been the first time in her life she had to face not just what alcohol had done to him, but what it could eventually do to her too.

Before things got really bad, they had moved in with me, Michael, and our kids, into our tiny two-bedroom apartment. My dad couldn't take care of himself anymore, and my mom was too weak and worn out to do it alone. So we were the ones left dealing with everything.

It's one thing to know the person you're with is dying. It's another to see your home start to look like a hospital.

I still remember the sound of my phone ringing. I didn't recognize the number, but I knew who it was. The delivery guy. I felt sick as I stared at the screen, holding my breath, knowing I couldn't ignore it. A deep voice came through—rough, accented—like he was just dropping off furniture. He said he was pulling up.

As the diesel engine got louder and stopped outside our window overlooking the lot, I looked away—I knew it was him. I thought about not answering the door, like if I ignored it, maybe none of it would be true.

Then the knock came. Firm. Unapologetic. I opened the door, and there it was. The hospital bed. The oxygen tanks. The tubing. The paperwork. He rolled it all in like he'd done it a hundred times before. Like it was no big deal.

But for us, it was the moment everything changed. There was no walking it back after that.

As he brought everything in, one piece at a time, my mom was already on her knees on the floor. She was falling apart. Tears streamed down her face—over her cheeks, down her neck, dripping onto her shirt. She couldn't think clearly. Couldn't say a word. She just stayed there, caught in how bad things had gotten, how real it all suddenly was.

Each piece looked like it had been dropped into the wrong place. Cold. Sterile. Mechanical. This was supposed to be a normal bedroom. A place to rest. To feel safe. And now it felt like the inside of a hospital room.

It made me think back to my own son's dying days—watching his small body propped up on the couch so he could breathe. We were always checking his heart rate and oxygen.

Dear Red Straw

I still remember the sounds. The steady beep of the monitor. The soft whoosh of the oxygen machine. The slow gurgle of the feeding pump. I used to sit there for hours, watching him. Wondering what would happen, when it would happen, and how I'd move forward after he was gone.

I imagine my mom felt many of those same things while she watched my dad. The helplessness. The quiet panic. That heavy sadness sitting in her chest.

But that day hit her especially hard. I could feel the fear behind her eyes—wanting someone to tell her this wasn't really happening. That maybe he'd get better. That this wasn't the end. That the disease wasn't going to keep taking everything that made him who he was.

And I think she knew, deep inside—if she didn't get a grip on her drinking, she might end up the same way.

But I was feeling done. Worn out. Tired of dealing with him. Tired of watching her drink all day. My whole life was getting pulled apart—so was Michael's and the kids'. My dad was always angry, paranoid, hard to be around because of the dementia. My mom wasn't doing any better. She was barely sleeping, and the drinking was only making it worse. And truthfully, I didn't care about their drinking anymore—I just wanted to live normally again.

As the weeks dragged on and my dad became harder to care for, it became clear that we all needed a break. So we put him in a care facility for a little while—

just a week or two so we could rest. Sleep. Get some strength back.

Right around then, my twin brother flew in to help with my mom. And the second he walked through the door, he saw it—how bad things had gotten. What we'd been living through. What our mom had become. He's not usually the one to take charge. Most of his life, he's been the anxious one—the one who lets others lead, who stays in the background. But this time was different.

Something in him changed. All the years of watching her drink, watching things fall apart—he hit a limit. And he didn't wait. He didn't ask. He just started moving.

He called and emailed every rehab center he could find. And in just a couple of days, he found one—about a hundred miles away—the only one that would take her insurance. He told her she was going. She didn't have a choice. And by the next day, she was gone.

She needed time. Space. A reset. He didn't ask if she was ready. He didn't have to. Watching what happened to my dad had already put sobriety on her mind—and that was enough.

Dear Red Straw

For the first time, my mom was in rehab. And for the first time, I let myself picture a future without alcohol in it. I had no idea how quickly that hope would fall apart.

I was used to how things normally went—sober during the day for work, drunk at night. It had gone on like that for so long, I couldn't picture anything else.

So of course, when my mom went to rehab, I didn't know what to think. Was she going to come home sober for good? What were the chances she'd start drinking again? What would she be like now, without the alcohol? Would she be a new person—happier, or more down? Would I need to watch her all the time, or would what she learned in rehab be enough to help her stay sober?

I hoped she'd come back with a new reason to live her life differently. That she'd spend her time doing better things—maybe helping others or reaching out to people again. I pictured her being more present, laughing with my kids, finding joy in the little things. Most of all, I hoped she wouldn't want to drink anymore. I really wanted to believe this would be her turning point.

I checked in with her every couple of days while she was in rehab. The place had tight rules about phone calls, and the only way to reach her was through a shared phone in the common room. Sometimes someone else was using it, or she'd be in a group meeting. It was hit or miss. But I didn't mind.

Jeremy Allen Damours

For the first time in a long time, I didn't have to worry—she was safe, being watched, and far away from alcohol.

But just when I let myself exhale, she opened her mouth and took it all back.

She wasn't even home yet. We were still driving back from rehab when she turned to me and said—

"I was wondering if you and I could have a drink to celebrate getting out of rehab."

I sat there stunned, hands on the wheel, the sun pouring through the windshield—hot and hazy, the air was heavy with dust. We were stuck at a red light, just two miles from home. Cars were everywhere—honking, switching lanes, inching forward—but I barely noticed. My mind was scattered. I didn't know what to think.

Did she really just say that?

I looked over at her, hoping I'd misunderstood. That maybe it was a joke. A bad one. But she was serious. Sitting there like it was the most normal thing in the world to ask your son for a drink the day you leave rehab.

"Are you serious?" I said, not even trying to hide the edge in my voice.

She shrugged, eyes a little wide—like she knew she shouldn't be asking, but said it anyway. Her face was tense, a little unsure. Like part of her was embarrassed, and part of her wasn't. "Just one," she said. "To celebrate. We've both been through a lot."

Dear Red Straw

I felt something sink in my chest. Like a door I thought was opening just slammed shut again.

This was supposed to be her turning point. Her moment. Her chance to fight for her life while Dad was losing his. We'd had so many conversations while she was in rehab—about her future, about how short life is, about doing better while there's still time. I believed her. I wanted to believe her.

I gripped the wheel tighter. Took a breath. Tried to keep my voice steady. "No, Mom. You just got out of rehab. You shouldn't be drinking again."

She looked away, staring straight ahead. Didn't say much. But the air between us felt heavy. Sick. I wanted to disappear. Anything but sit in that silence.

I wanted her to hear more than just the word no. I wanted her to understand how much I still cared. How badly I wanted her to get this right—for all of us.

"This can't be happening," I mouthed quietly. "I can't believe this is happening."

We didn't talk about it anymore. But I knew something else was coming. I could feel it.

The next day, my aunt flew into town to surprise her. She was proud my mom had finished rehab. We ended up going to the beach that afternoon to celebrate—not expecting what would happen next, at least not so soon.

As soon as we got to the beach, my mom—who usually moved slow because of her back—suddenly walked off. Quick. Quiet. She didn't say anything. None of us saw it. We'd only turned around for a minute. By the time we looked up, she was gone—already lost in the crowd.

We took off after her, heading toward the bars. It was the first place that came to mind.

Minutes passed. Then ten. Then twenty. We kept scanning faces, brushing past people, hoping she'd show up. I couldn't believe she'd gotten that far. At one point, I almost turned around, sure we'd missed her—but something in me said to keep going.

As I kept walking, I couldn't stop thinking about the day before. About what she said in the car. Asking me to drink with her—right after rehab. I didn't want to believe she meant it. I wanted to think it was a weird moment. A slip. But now it felt like she'd meant every word.

And then, just ahead of me, I saw it. A bar and grill with a big outdoor patio—and there she was. Sitting alone at a table, menu in hand. She hadn't ordered yet, but it looked like she was about to.

But her face stopped me. She didn't look restless like I'd expected after the way she'd walked off. She looked...lonely. Like something in her was about to give up. Like there was a quiet fight happening behind her eyes. She looked like she wanted to order a drink—but something was holding her back.

That's when it hit me. She hadn't just wandered off. She was trying to figure something out. Maybe part of her really did want a drink—but part of her was still trying to do the right thing. It looked like both sides were pulling at her at the same time.

Dear Red Straw

I sat down next to her without saying much. No arguing. No judging. Just small talk, like none of it had just happened. A few minutes later, my brother and aunt showed up and joined us. Still, no one said a word about it.

I think we were scared to say anything. We didn't want to push her too far. We were probably hoping she'd be strong enough to say no without us stepping in. But that didn't make it go away—it was still there between us, and none of us could ignore it.

We were holding onto hope, but she was already slipping through our fingers.

Jeremy Allen Damours

But relapse doesn't always start with the drink. Sometimes, it starts with loneliness. With too much time, too many temptations, and not enough of the right people around you.

After the bar and grill incident on the beach, things seemed—well, normal at first. There were no signs she was drinking again. And as the days came and went, I started to wonder if maybe I had made too big a deal out of her asking for that drink right after she got out. Maybe it was just a mistake—not a sign she was going to fall back into it.

As far as I could tell, she wasn't drinking in secret. Every day, she'd tell us what day of sobriety she was on—either out loud or in group texts she sent to the family. And knowing my mom, I figured if she had started again, the guilt would've made her stop sending those messages. Things seemed to be going in the right direction. And for the first time in a long time, I stopped watching her so closely.

But just as we were all starting to feel comfortable again, things began to change. After my dad died, my mom seemed lonelier by the day. She started talking about dating again—wanting the kind of closeness that comes from being with someone.

The problem was, she had never really dated before. She met my dad in school when she was fifteen, and that was it. And people weren't meeting at burger joints or house parties anymore. These days, most of it happened online—through social media and dating apps, where meeting someone new was just a few clicks away.

My mom didn't drive, so social media became her main way of seeing what was out there. It was easy to use and always within reach. Before long, she was getting tons of messages from men—most of them either after sex or trying to scam her for money.

Even outside of the apps, men noticed her. Grocery store workers, rideshare drivers—even a guy in the meat department slipped her his number once. There was always someone trying to get close. And none of them cared that she was trying to stay sober.

Some were heavy drinkers, some used drugs, and others just didn't think it mattered. They weren't going to stop for her. They wanted the alcohol, and they wanted her body.

My mom, still hurting and not good at setting limits, didn't know how to say no.

My brothers and I tried to help. We warned her about the men she was talking to and told her they didn't seem like good guys. But she didn't listen. She kept talking to them anyway, convinced she could handle things on her own.

Some of these guys called her beautiful. Told her they missed her. Some said they loved her. Asked about her day. That kind of attention made her feel wanted.

And slowly, they became what she cared about most. Not her sobriety. Not her health. Just the feeling they gave her. That's what opened the door again.

She didn't stop talking about being sober all at once. It just came up less and less—until one day, it didn't come up at all. Then her behavior started to change.

She kept asking if everything was okay. If we were mad at her. She got overly sweet, overly apologetic—like she was trying hard not to upset us. That's how she gets when she's drinking.

When she's sober, she's steadier. More like herself. She doesn't keep checking to see if we're okay with her, or need us to keep telling her she's not doing anything wrong.

And this time, she wasn't acting like that.

When I started to think she might be drinking again, I began paying more attention—especially to how she handled her trash. That's when I noticed she'd stopped using the kitchen garbage and started taking her bedroom trash straight to the outside bin.

One day, after she dropped off a bag and went back to her room, I went outside, lifted the lid, and found what I had already guessed—empty bottles of Long Island Iced Tea.

I wasn't surprised—but I was still furious. I already knew, but seeing the bottles made it real. What hurt most was the lying. I had asked her before, more than once, if she'd been feeling tempted, and she'd always said no.

And I felt betrayed—like everything we'd already been through meant nothing. Like she had forgotten all the pain, everything it had done to us, and

Dear Red Straw

was just doing it all over again. I wanted to storm up to her room and scream.

But I didn't. I calmed myself down. Yelling wouldn't help.

If I wanted even a chance for her to be honest—for her to actually admit it—I couldn't go in yelling. I had to stay calm and think about how to handle it. I had to be careful.

Because as much as I still cared and wanted her to get better, I wasn't just trying to fix her anymore. I was trying to protect us—Michael, our kids, and myself.

At first, she kept saying no—over and over—with that same look, like she was surprised and had no idea why I was asking.

I didn't show her the bottles right away. I stood there, waiting—giving her chance after chance to just say it. Not because I caught her, but because she knew I already knew.

She sat on the edge of her bed, looking into my eyes—didn't blink, didn't look away. Like she was thinking hard about what to say while trying to keep a straight face. Then she looked away, still wearing that same look, like she was sticking to her story. A few seconds later, she looked back.

"I haven't had anything to drink," she said, voice flat. "I swear."

I didn't answer right away. I just stood there, staring at her. My heart was beating fast, but my face stayed calm.

"Are you sure?" I said, my voice low. "Because I already know, Mom."

She shook her head. "No no no no no, I'm not drinking. I promise. I wouldn't do that."

My teeth clenched, frustration crawling up my chest. I didn't say anything.

So I walked out of the room, grabbed the trash bag from outside, came back in, and set it on the floor between us.

Suddenly, her face changed. Her eyes widened. She knew the lie was done, and there was no way to keep it going.

Dear Red Straw

She promised it wouldn't happen again. Swore she'd do better. And I wanted to believe her. But what came next wasn't relief. It was something messier. Something harder to see.

Not long after that talk, I noticed she was taking longer naps and sleeping more during the day. She looked groggy—like she was on something. When I asked her about it, she said she'd started taking more of one of her pills but couldn't remember which one.

The doctors already had her on a mix of things—meds for her mood, pain, swelling, allergies—even Benadryl to help her sleep. After a while, I started to wonder if she was trading the drinking for pills. Or maybe just adding them to it.

Then she started falling. Once, twice, then more often. One fall hit the same spot on her back where she'd had surgery a year or two earlier. I started to feel more like a babysitter than her son—always watching her. Some nights I had to tell her to stay in her room, just so she wouldn't get hurt.

There were a couple of nights when things got so bad, I had to call an ambulance. She'd be slurring her words, barely able to stand—staring at the floor like she couldn't bring herself to look up.

One time, she was at the bottom of the stairs, hunched over, trying to get to her room. "Help me," she kept saying. "I don't know what's wrong."

Jeremy Allen Damours

I asked her again and again— "Mom, what's wrong?" "Did you take something?" "Have you been drinking?" But she wouldn't answer. Or couldn't. She'd start to talk, then stop halfway through, like I was supposed to fill in the rest.

The whole time, she kept reaching for the railing like she was going to pull herself up—then letting go again. Like she was confused. Or too weak. Getting to her room seemed to be the only thing on her mind, like if she could just get away from me, maybe I wouldn't notice how bad it really was. She wanted help, but she didn't want to admit she needed it.

I'd gotten her up the stairs—barely.

She couldn't let go of the railing, stopping on every stair to get her strength back. I knew I wouldn't be able to carry her. But when we finally reached the top—out of nowhere—she got a sudden burst of energy and lurched down the hallway toward her bedroom.

But before I could catch up to her, she tripped.

Her body slammed into the bed, landing awkward—half on, half off. She didn't cry out. Didn't groan. Just laid there.

"I'm fine," she mumbled. "Really, I'm fine. Don't worry about me."

I leaned over and asked if she was okay. Begged her to tell me if she'd taken anything.

She didn't answer. Just kept saying, "I'm okay, I'm okay."

Dear Red Straw

That's when I knew. I didn't know what she'd taken. Pills? Alcohol? Both? Something else? I had no idea. And I couldn't keep guessing. I couldn't believe what she told me anymore, couldn't wait to see if she'd sleep it off like all the other times. The moment the paramedics took her; I felt this strange mix of relief and guilt. Relief because—for at least a day or two—she'd be someone else's problem. Guilt because I didn't follow the ambulance. I wasn't planning to sit in the ER for hours or watch her detox in a hospital bed. She wouldn't even remember I was there.

And it wasn't about being seen. It was about survival—mine.

I needed space. I needed to take care of Michael, our kids, and my own mental health.

I needed to come up for air.

Michael tried to understand, but he couldn't. To him, it looked like I didn't care. And maybe he wasn't wrong.

But this wasn't the first time.

I'd been through it before. At the hospital, I'd tell the staff about her drinking so they could prep for withdrawal—or even seizures and confusion if it got bad.

If I was there, I'd fix the lies she told during intake. If I wasn't, I'd end up calling later to explain it all again. As a nurse, I knew how it worked. That didn't make it easier. It was the same routine every time. Same story. Same fake reassurances.

It wore me down.

Jeremy Allen Damours

Bottle after bottle, lie after lie, something in me finally let go. Not out of anger—just done.

Nothing I did was getting through to her, so I stopped trying to control her drinking. I stopped trying to save her. I had quietly started to make peace with the idea that this was just how things were going to be. Maybe not forever, but for now.

I didn't feel good about that, but I didn't feel bad either. I couldn't keep putting myself through it. I'd done everything I could.

So when I found more bottles in the trash one day, I walked into her room. Just like always, it took forever to get her to admit it—but she finally did.

"I'm not going to try to stop you anymore," I said. "I just can't do it. If you can't keep it under control, you'll need to move out."

She didn't get angry. She just looked at me, caught off guard—like she couldn't believe I actually meant it. "Now that you told me I can drink," she said, "it makes me not want to anymore."

For a second, I thought she might've meant it.

That feeling didn't last long. Within the week, she flew out to Texas to visit my brother and his family. Said she needed a break from everything—really, she needed a break from me.

She spent a few days there. I didn't know it at the time, but while she was visiting, the idea of moving

Dear Red Straw

in came up. They offered. I don't think they knew what they were getting into—because they hadn't been living with what I had. They hadn't seen how hard it had gotten.

When she came back, she didn't say much. Just acted like it was a quick visit, like nothing had changed. But something had. She was quieter than usual. Less attitude. No arguing. She kept to herself, like something was already turning in her head.

Then, a few mornings later, she just looked at me and said it—she was moving in with them, and she'd already bought her ticket back to Texas.

At first, it stung. After everything Michael and I had done—for her, for my dad when he was dying, for the years after—this felt like a shrug. Like it didn't matter. And now she was leaving.

Part of me felt like I could finally breathe. I had let go. But deep down, I didn't want to.

I told her it was a bad idea. That it wouldn't be the change she was hoping for. That she had more help here than she'd ever get over there.

They had full days. Busy lives. They worked, traveled. My mom wasn't going to get the kind of help she was used to. She liked doing whatever she wanted—but still wanted someone around. Someone noticing. Someone paying attention. Not to question her or get in the way—just to be there. And that wasn't going to happen.

But she was angry. Fed up. And when she saw a way out, she took it. It was easier than facing everything she'd broken here.

I didn't try to stop her. I'd already let go. And deep down, I think she knew it.

Sure enough, the move didn't change anything. She spent a couple of years in Texas falling back into the same habits—just under a different roof. Her drinking didn't stop, and her health kept getting worse. Her back got so bad she could barely walk, and it had started to curve so much it was making it harder for her to breathe.

There was no choice left but to put a rod down her spine. It was a big surgery—and a risky one.

I flew out to Texas to be there. I didn't know what I'd see—but I wasn't ready for how bad it was. When I walked in and saw her, I felt sick. She looked completely broken. Thin. Faded. Face sunken in.

She looked just like her own mother had near the end—used up by years of alcohol. I stood there, staring. It was like looking into the future and the past at the same time. And it hit me—drinking had done this to her.

I wasn't sure she'd make it through the surgery. And even if she did, I didn't know how much longer her body could take it. It was hard to look at her. Hard to believe how far things had gone. Still, a part of me hoped—hoped that if she pulled through, maybe this would finally be it. Maybe she'd stop drinking.

I sat in the waiting room for ten hours, expecting bad news. But somehow, when the doctor came out, he

Dear Red Straw

said she made it. The surgery went well. I felt relief. And disbelief. I'd spent all day getting ready to hear the worst… and it didn't happen.

But just when I thought the hardest part was over, something else came to mind.

I'd forgotten to mention she was an alcoholic when her nurse made an offhand comment about how confused she was getting. I'd noticed it too, but figured it was just the pain meds.

That's when I knew. She was in withdrawal.

She spent weeks in the hospital, barely there. Her whole body wouldn't stop shaking. She couldn't talk. Couldn't eat. Couldn't sit up. She was tied to the bed. Her words came out like broken pieces that didn't make sense.

She looked small. Sunken. Her eyes were open, but nothing was in them. Like she was stuck between here and somewhere else.

And more than once, I stood there wondering if this was it. If she was going to die. Or if this was the moment that would take her mind for good.

Jeremy Allen Damours

But somehow—she pulled through. Barely.

And when she finally came back to herself, she said she was ready to start over. That she was serious this time. That she was done.

I wanted to believe her. I really did. I sat there, nodding, telling her I was glad. And I was. I was glad she was awake. Glad she was alive. Glad she could talk again.

But part of me had heard it too many times. And I hated that. Hated how hard it had gotten to believe her. Hated how numb I'd started to feel.

After everything… I just didn't know anymore.

She stayed sober for a while after that. Maybe longer than ever before.

She moved into a small apartment. She didn't love it, but it gave her space—and gave the rest of us room to breathe. For a while, things were steady. Not great. But quiet.

And then she started drinking again. Just a little at first.

None of us said anything. We didn't want to lose the calm we'd finally found.

But deep down, I knew what was coming. We all did.

Dear Red Straw

Relapse doesn't always look the same. Sometimes it's easy to see. The drinking. The way they act. Other times, it's quiet. They pull back. Seem tired. Distant. They stop being around. Stop doing the things that were helping for a while. You ask if something's wrong—they say they're fine. But you feel it. Something's off. And you know.

Sometimes you see it before they do. You watch it happening—little things at first—but they brush it off. Tell you you're overthinking. And you start to wonder if maybe you are. But deep down, you know. Even when you try to push it aside, it stays. That quiet sense that they're unraveling.

And that's the part people don't always talk about. What it takes out of you to keep loving someone who keeps falling back. The guilt. The anger. The deep care. The love that won't let go, even when walking away would be easier.

At times, I didn't know which emotion would win. I felt all of them—sometimes all at once. Not perfectly. Not always gracefully. But I stayed—because underneath the heaviness, I still wanted to believe my mom would find her way back.

And maybe that's what this has all come down to: not just the weight of relapse, but the weight of loving someone through it.

Jeremy Allen Damours

Dear Mom,

I don't think you really know how proud I am of you.

Not because you're ignoring it, but because I probably haven't said it in a way that really gets through. I've tried, but I don't think I've said it clearly enough, or in a way that matches how big it feels inside me. I wish I could say it better. I wish you could feel what I feel when I say it. Because it's not small. It's not surface-level. It's deep. It's real.

I'm proud of you for being sober these last 180 days. I'm proud of you for sticking with it even when it would've been easier not to. And I'm proud of you for showing up every day—even the days you probably didn't want to. I mean that.

But if I'm honest, part of what holds me back from showing more emotion when I say it is fear. I worry that if I get too excited, or let my guard down too much, I'll stop being what I think I need to be for you. And I put that guard up for a reason. It's not to

Dear Red Straw

punish you. It's not to withhold love. It's to protect both of us. I think you know that.

I know sometimes it feels like I'm being too serious, too reserved, like I can't just enjoy things with you. But that guard is there for a reason. I can't be the friend who just goes along with whatever you want, or the one who agrees with you just to keep the peace. I also can't be the guy who's serious all the time and never lets you have any fun. It's like I have to be all of those people, depending on the moment. Because there aren't a lot of other people in your life playing those roles. And maybe I don't have to be that person—but I choose to be. I'm still here because I want to be here.

You've told me more than once that you're lucky any of us still talk to you after everything that's happened. And you're right. You are lucky. A lot of people in your shoes have lost everyone. Some bridges don't get rebuilt. But you've got people in your life who still care. Who still want to see you win. And I hope you never forget that.

Jeremy Allen Damours

And Mom—you should be proud of yourself too. You've stayed sober. You've fought temptation. You've gone to your group every week. You've kept yourself accountable—sending me those drug screen results every night. You've taken real steps. You're not trying to do it alone anymore. That matters. That shows growth. That shows heart.

You've done something Dad never did. Something he didn't want to do. You're doing the work that he wouldn't even try. And maybe part of him didn't want you to get better—because if you got better, it would mean letting go of him. Letting go of that shared addiction. I don't say that to make him the villain. I know you had your own choices too. But you broke free. You let go. You're building something new now.

You are free of alcohol.

You are free of his grip on you.

You are free to live your own damn life.

Keep going, Mom. Keep being free.

CHAPTER 10

WHEN DEATH MOVES IN

I've spent almost 20 years of my nursing career watching people die. Not every day, but often enough. Death found its way into the rooms, hallways, and homes I worked in—sometimes expected, sometimes not.

But my first experience with death came before I ever became a nurse. I watched my son die in his sleep just after his first birthday, after months of slowly withering from Menkes disease. His life—and his death—are what led me into nursing.

One of my first patients was a man in his sixties, a heavy smoker and alcoholic, who ended up at the care home where I worked not long after I finished nursing school. He had a lung disease so bad he couldn't walk across the room without gasping for air. The stuff he coughed up was so thick I could turn the cup upside down and nothing would spill—like silly putty stuck to the bottom. I remember hearing the doctor tell him he was too far gone for new lungs. Six to nine months left, at best.

One evening, he was having a hard time breathing. I kept telling the nurse in charge—a nurse who'd been doing this a long time and had seen this kind of dying before. After walking the hall with me a few times to check on him, she finally said, "He's circling the drain. Stop checking his vital signs." She wasn't trying to be mean. Just honest.

We checked on him throughout the night, and he died not long after.

There were others, too.

One I still think about was a woman in her late forties with brain cancer that was going to kill her.

I was her home health nurse for a while, visiting twice a week to clean and wrap the sores on her legs—left over from the radiation they'd done all over her body. She didn't trust anyone. She was angry. Mad that she was dying, and no one could stop it.

Almost every time I came—whether we were talking or I was changing her wraps—she'd be sitting there smoking, like it was the one thing she still had control over.

After a while, she started getting weaker. She began forgetting things. Struggled to find her words. Walking became harder, until she couldn't do it at all.

She spent most of her time lying down and had to use a bedside bucket when she needed to go. But even when her thinking got cloudy, she still tried to get up on her own. Still tried to say what she needed to say. She fell a lot and hurt herself, but she wasn't ready to let go. Her body was breaking down, but her will to live wouldn't quit.

I left that job before she died, but I still think about her. I don't know why she's stayed with me all

Dear Red Straw

these years. Maybe because her fight was so raw. So human. She didn't want to die. Her denial ran deeper than her body's limits. Seeing her lose everything, piece by piece, made me feel small. Fragile. Helpless.

It reminded me how close we all are to the end. Death doesn't wait for us to be ready. And it doesn't care how much we still want to live.

That's just the truth.

We're all going to die. We don't get to choose how or when. And the harder people are on their bodies, the harder the dying tends to be.

It doesn't care how old you are, what dreams you haven't finished, or who you are in this world.

And maybe the hardest part is that death isn't what we pretend it is. We try to make it look easier. But it's not.

We tell ourselves it's peaceful—a gentle, spiritual passing—because the truth is harder to face. But in reality, death starts long before someone dies. It's messy. It smells. It drains. It rattles. It can be painful to witness and even more painful to experience. We don't talk about that part enough, because it's easier not to.

And because we don't, people end up feeling shocked, alone, or ashamed when it finally comes.

But even knowing all of this—everything I'd sat through with patients over the years—it felt different when it was my dad.

The changes didn't come all at once. At first, they were easy to blame on getting older, stress, or drinking. He'd forget things. Seem off. Move a little slower. Nothing that felt serious. Nothing we thought much about. Still, something big was already changing in him. We just didn't know it yet.

Dear Red Straw

Watching strangers die is one thing. Watching someone you love slowly disappear is another.

I saw it in pieces.

And those pieces don't always make sense at first. Sometimes they come as whispers—quiet, barely-there hints that something's off. I started noticing them the year before my dad died, when Michael and I asked my parents to come see us in Florida. The idea of getting out of the Alaskan cold—forty below—for some sun was hard to say no to. And when they got there, everything felt normal. Familiar. Like any other visit.

But after a couple of days, I could tell something wasn't quite right.

My parents normally got up early, and they always made their bed—every morning, no matter what. That didn't change just because they were staying at our place. But each day, when I walked past the room they were using, the bed was only halfway done. The blanket looked like it had been pulled up with one hand on each side, then left. The sheets were crooked, wrinkled in the middle—not smoothed out the way they usually kept things.

I stood there, looking at it—trying to make sense of it. It wasn't laziness. It wasn't forgetfulness. Whoever made that bed hadn't had the energy to finish. Not even enough to tug a light sheet into place. I didn't know what it meant, but it didn't feel right.

Jeremy Allen Damours

It reminded me of how my kids used to make their beds—like they tried, but left it halfway. Only this time, it wasn't about effort.

I didn't say anything. But I kept thinking about it.

And it wasn't just that.

Every time we went out—whether it was the beach, the grocery store, or just seeing the sights—my dad had to stop and rest more than usual. Sometimes we weren't even out long. A lot of the time, it was just quick runs for more alcohol and bagged ice. But even then, he kept saying his legs felt "weak." Not sore. Not tired. Not achy. Just weak.

And that wasn't a word he used often. My dad didn't like showing weakness—especially not in a way people could see. He cared about how he looked to others. He didn't want to seem fragile. Or like he couldn't handle things.

It got even stranger when I took them to the Everglades for an airboat ride.

It was one of those perfect days—sunny, dry, not too hot. Before the boat ride, we made our way past some big alligators stretched out in the sun. They didn't move, just lay there with their jaws tightly closed, like they were half-asleep but still watching. Off to the side, a baby gator rested in a small pen. Someone said we could pet it later.

Not far from that were a few giant turtles, parked in the dirt with their shells rough and worn, like old stone baking in the heat. They didn't seem bothered.

Dear Red Straw

Near the fence, a guy was talking to a small group—something about the animals, maybe the land. I wasn't really listening. But what happened next didn't feel like just the alcohol.

When it was time to climb down into the boat, I watched my dad—and he just stopped. Froze, like he forgot what he was doing halfway through.

He looked almost lost as he gripped the rail. Eyes dull—just kind of staring, not the usual buzzed or tipsy look I knew so well. This was something else. His body looked stuck—like he was inside it, but not steering it. Like his brain was telling it what to do, and it just wasn't doing it.

It felt wrong. He wasn't okay. Not just tired or weak. I couldn't put my finger on it.

The ride was beautiful. Open water, sawgrass, birds flying across the sky. One of the guides talked about how the Everglades helps supply the drinking water—how it keeps things going.

But the whole time, all I could think about was my dad sitting in front of me. I kept watching the back of his head. He just stared out, not really tuned in. Just... there. Like a passenger in his own body.

As we pulled into the dock, it happened again. He couldn't get out of the boat on his own. He put his hands on the cold metal sides and tried to push himself up. Nothing. He tried again. And again. Little efforts that didn't get him anywhere. The worker waited, giving him a chance to do it on his own. But it wasn't working, so he took him by the arms and helped him up. His legs were shaky. Weak. He didn't say a word.

Jeremy Allen Damours

That was the first time I didn't just see my dad as the man who brought me up. I saw him as someone... slower, smaller, not all there. And I didn't know what to do with it. The way I'd always seen him in my head was the one who worked every day without fail, no matter what job he had. Even when things were bad—when he was drinking, when things felt off at home—he still made sure we had food, heat, a roof. He still protected us.

And now here he was, needing help to step out of a boat. The image I'd held onto all these years was breaking down in front of me

One night, just before they flew home, we went out to dinner—and it got more uncomfortable by the minute.

My dad had been drinking before we got there, like always. As we sat waiting for our food, his voice started getting louder. He sounded a little mean. He'd blurt things out without thinking—small put-downs, complaints, stuff that didn't need to be said but came out anyway.

But this time, he kept going. One comment turned into another, and then another.

First, it was the drinks. Said they were taking too long, even though they came out in just a few minutes. He kept looking around, bothered—like something wasn't right, even though everything was fine. Then the food. Said it was bad, even though he'd just said it tasted pretty good. One chewy bite of steak, and suddenly the whole night was ruined. He pushed his plate away like he was mad at it.

Dear Red Straw

Then the check showed up, and there was no senior discount.

That was it.

I told him I'd pay, that it was my treat. But it didn't matter. He grabbed the check and started waving it around, yelling for the waitress to come fix it. Loud. Rude. Like it was personal.

It threw me a little—but I didn't dwell on it. Just felt uncomfortable and a little confused. He'd acted like that before, but only at home. So I let it go.

I didn't put it together that night—not the way I had on the airboat. It would take a few more months before it all made sense.

That's when I stopped being able to pretend everything was fine.

Jeremy Allen Damours

The second they got back, I knew we weren't just dealing with a bad week.

They'd only been home a month when my mom called me. She was worried—said my dad was getting weaker. That wasn't like him. He never missed work unless something serious was going on. So when he started saying he couldn't lift boxes on freight days, or that stocking shelves was getting too hard, she knew it wasn't nothing.

So did I.

At first, we thought maybe it was just age—or burnout. But it wasn't going away. And it wasn't getting better.

He started going from doctor to doctor, but no one could figure out what was wrong. And when they asked if he smoked or drank, neither of my parents told the truth. He never once said he was a heavy drinker, and my mom always backed him up. They told the story they wanted the doctors to believe.

They did every kind of test—blood work, brain scans, ultrasounds, even cutting into his muscle to look for answers. But everything kept coming back normal. And still, he kept getting weaker.

They ruled out things like muscle and nerve diseases. But after enough dead ends, it felt like the doctors were giving up. Like they didn't know what to do with him anymore, so they stopped trying. They acted like if the tests were fine, then he was fine too.

Dear Red Straw

Nobody looked deeper. No one asked about the drinking, because no one knew. They were all treating the version of him he wanted them to see.

But the change was impossible to ignore.

Six months later, new scans told a different story—his brain was smaller. Sick. Wasting away.

And if falling apart one way wasn't enough—now he couldn't swallow right. He'd choke on his food—not every meal, but often enough to notice. It came out of nowhere, for no reason anyone could figure out.

Then he did something I never thought I'd see.

He had just gotten dressed for work and was about to leave when he stopped. He stood there for a few seconds—right in the open doorway—his silhouette lit by the early light, facing the cold.

The sun was just starting to rise, casting its soft rays through the bare, snow-covered trees. Shadows from the branches stretched across the porch. Light hit the snow in scattered patches—like millions of tiny shards of glass. Everything else stayed still. Quiet. Like the world was about to hold its breath.

My mom could feel it—something was happening. He wasn't just standing there.

It was like his body knew what his mind didn't want to say.

He'd spent his whole life working. It wasn't just what he did—it was who he was. Sick, hungover, didn't matter. He went. Because work wasn't about money. It gave him routine. Something that made him feel useful. A reason to get out of bed.

And now, in that pause at the door, I think he knew—his body had turned on him. And maybe that was the hardest part to face: That the man who always kept going… couldn't anymore. That this was becoming who he was now.

He turned around. Looked at my mom.

And said, "I can't do this anymore."

That was it. He had nothing left. The man who never gave up had finally surrendered to his body.

He never worked another day after that.

Dear Red Straw

They couldn't do it anymore—not physically, not financially. And deep down, I think we all knew what that meant.

So they came to live with us—at least, for a while. We were hoping the doctors here could figure out what was wrong. My dad still believed we'd get answers—that this was just a bump in the road, that things would go back to normal. That he'd go back to Alaska.

But I didn't believe that. Not really. I wanted to—I nodded along, said all the right things—but inside, I felt it coming. Whatever was happening to him felt unstoppable. Like watching a slow collapse. This wasn't something we were going to fix. It was something we were going to watch take him. I just didn't know when—or how long it would be.

When they got here, I saw it right away. They both looked weaker than they had just a few months before. My mom needed a wheelchair sometimes—not because she couldn't walk at all, but because she didn't have the energy to go very far. And while my dad was still walking on his own, it was clear his body was giving out. I could tell by the way he moved—slower, shakier, like he didn't fully trust his legs anymore.

Neither of them could work. And they just couldn't take care of each other. They needed help, and we were the only ones who could be there for them.

Jeremy Allen Damours

I knew it wouldn't be easy. But I didn't know how hard it was about to get—or how much it would cost Michael and the kids along the way.

To make space, the kids' beds went into the living room. Shoved side by side in front of the TV—right out in the open, like furniture.

They tried to turn it into something better. Threw sheets over the sides. Hung up clothes like curtains. Built little tents out of whatever they could find—anything to make a spot that felt even a little bit their own. But it wasn't the same.

They didn't have a door to close anymore. No quiet place to hide. No space to play a game, stretch out, and just be a kid. That was gone.

And I felt awful about that.

And still, they didn't complain. But I could see it—the way they grew quieter, how they talked less, held more in. It got harder to understand them. Like cocoons refusing to open, even after their time had come. Whatever was inside had given up on coming out—tucked in too tight, not even sure what they were supposed to do with everything they were feeling.

They had to lie there, night after night, while the house stayed wide awake. Someone always up, walking through the kitchen—grabbing snacks, opening drawers, letting cabinets slam shut. Normal stuff, maybe. But not at midnight. Not with two kids trying to sleep a few feet away, on beds squeezed into the living room that didn't belong there.

Dear Red Straw

And then there was the drinking. My parents moved through the dark like clockwork—every couple of hours, heading to the freezer for more ice. No lights on. Just the freezer door cracking open, cubes hitting glass, the soft scrape of their steps across the tile, fading back into the night. It wasn't loud. But it was enough to keep you awake. Enough to remind you who everything was still about.

The kids lay there through all of it—eyes closed, backs turned, pretending it didn't matter.

But I know it did.

Even the ice maker started to give out.

It just stopped working one day—like it couldn't keep up with all the drinking.

That's when the ice runs started. We bought bags almost every day, filling the freezer with as much as it could hold. But it never lasted. If we ran out too fast, it meant another trip to the gas station or grocery store—no matter what time it was.

One night, we ran out of ice again.

"Can you take me?" she asked, trying to stand—already a little off.

She was drunk, probably had taken too many pills, and hadn't slept in days from taking care of my dad. But she still looked put together—clean clothes, tidy hair. It was everything underneath that gave her away. She walked slow, dragging a little, like it was hard just to keep going. Her body leaned forward a bit, like she was trying to stay standing but didn't really care if she could.

Jeremy Allen Damours

I drove us to the gas station and parked out front. I didn't want to go in—I was tired, fed up with the drinking, and didn't feel like doing one more thing I wished she could do on her own. So I stayed in the car and let her go inside. The windows stretched across the whole front of the store, so I could see everything from where I was.

She slowly made her way to the freezer, trying not to fall with each step. She grabbed a bag that looked lighter—the only one sitting right on top of one of the piles, the easy one—without even noticing the hole near the bottom corner. As she turned to go pay, ice fell out behind her in a loose trail, and by the time she got to the counter, a thin line of water had traced her steps like a quiet creek.

She plopped the half-empty bag on the counter. Didn't notice the hole. Didn't notice the water. Didn't notice the ice still falling out.

I looked away and let out a tired breath. "Whatever. Just get it over with."

The clerk stared at her. I could see his face from the car—confused, a little startled, like he didn't know if he should laugh or help. He pointed toward the bag, then gestured toward the freezer. I couldn't hear the words, but I could guess.

"Hang on, let me get you a full one," probably.

My mom didn't say a word. Just stood there, swaying slightly, while he walked away. Her face looked empty. No hint she felt anything. Just a woman in clean clothes, stuck in a body that couldn't handle it anymore.

Dear Red Straw

When he handed her the new bag, she took it and walked back out like nothing had happened.

I'd been watching this my whole life. But that day, I looked at her and knew—this wasn't just bad. There's a real problem here.

After that, they needed something from me all the time. Day, night—it never stopped.

I was working from home every day and the constant stopping and starting was wearing me out.

She'd come to me needing something—usually about my dad. Sometimes it was help opening pill bottles or cans. Sometimes it was making a doctor's appointment or trying to look something up on the computer.

Other times, she just needed to talk. About how hard it was. About the things he said. The way he moved. How forgetful he was getting. She paid close attention to everything—his breathing, his words, even the way he sat still—watching for signs that he was getting worse.

Didn't matter if I was on a call. If she needed something, she came to me.

And when she wasn't home—off in a rideshare for groceries or a doctor's visit—he was left with me. That's when he'd start to lose it.

"God damn it, Kathy!" he'd yell from the bedroom. I knew he was struggling with his phone, trying to call her—pressing the wrong buttons, swearing, getting more upset by the second.

Jeremy Allen Damours

I'd be in the middle of talking on a work call, trying to keep my voice calm while I reached for the mute button, hoping no one could hear him yelling behind me. It felt like living two lives at once—one on screen, holding it together, and the other behind me, coming apart in plain sight.

And if I didn't go calm him down, he'd end up staggering into my room—confused, angry, looking for her.

"Where's Mom? God damn it, Kathy!"

He'd stand in the doorway, yelling. I'd quickly turn my camera off and try to take him back to his room. If he wouldn't go, I'd grab my phone and fake a call—pretending I was talking to my mom, then hang up and tell him her ride was pulling up and she couldn't talk. Sometimes he'd believe me and go back. Other times, I'd just have to wait it out, sitting there with him behind me until he finally left.

I always felt better when my mom got home. She could calm him when I couldn't.

But I saw it in her face every time she walked through the door—like she was already somewhere else. Like she didn't want to be here anymore.

She was worn out.

Taking care of him, and trying to hold herself together, had turned into something that was breaking her down.

And even after the workday ended, it didn't stop.

Dear Red Straw

Michael and the kids would come home after work and school to find my parents already drunk—going around and around with the same stories, the same gripes about who had wronged my dad, the same talk about moving back to Alaska, getting on disability, or going back to work—plans we all knew weren't going to happen. It never went anywhere.

And Michael… I started to see him change. Bit by bit. He got quieter. Kept more to himself. He walked through the apartment with that look on his face—the one that said, don't bother me. Barely spoke. Just did what he had to do and nothing more.

He started coming home later. He'd take the long way back. Make extra stops. Anything to keep from walking through the door. And when he did come in, he'd go right to our room and close the door behind him. Some nights, he didn't come back out at all.

Home didn't feel like home anymore—for either of us. But at least he had a door to close. A way to get away from it. I didn't. I was the one everyone came to—for my parents, for the kids. There was nowhere I could go to be alone. No break from the pressure. No break from the slow, sinking feeling that everything was wrong.

And then there was the guilt. My mom would give me a hard time whenever I stayed in my room too long. She thought I was staying away from her—and I was. But not just her. I was staying away from both of them—on purpose.

"Is everything okay? I noticed you were in your room." "You went in without saying hello—is everything okay between us?" "You and Michael have been in your room all night. Did we upset you all?" "You're being quiet… is everything alright?"

I needed space. I needed to breathe without being asked for something, without being needed, without someone knocking, calling, asking for help the second I sat down.

I missed myself. I missed Michael. I missed the boys. And I didn't know how to get any of us back.

And it was my fault. I brought this into our home. Their addiction, their mess, their problems—and let it take over the home I'd tried so hard to hold together for Michael and the kids. A place that once felt like ours started to feel like it wasn't. Like we were just getting by.

It couldn't go on like that.

Dear Red Straw

But the madness didn't stop. Even without a diagnosis, we could feel it.

Something was coming.

One of the hardest things between my parents during all of this was the one thing they couldn't agree on—death.

While we didn't have any answers yet, my mom could feel it. Deep down, she knew he didn't have much time left. Even as she held onto hope that doctors might find a cure or a way to slow things down, I could see her preparing for what was coming.

She needed him to face what was happening. To say it out loud so she wouldn't feel so alone in knowing he was dying.

She'd try to talk to him—ask questions, ease into it, hoping to get a sense of what he felt deep down. Whether he was scared. Whether he saw what she saw. Whether he was ready.

In her own way, she needed him to be strong for her. To tell her it would be okay. That he'd be waiting for her.

She wanted comfort from the very person she was about to lose.

But my dad wouldn't talk about it. And when she tried to bring it up, he'd cut her off. He'd ignore her or yell at her to shut up. She'd cry. They'd fight. Nothing ever got worked out.

He wasn't thinking clearly—his brain was already damaged from the drinking. And he didn't have it in him to comfort her, to talk through what was happening, or to admit what they both knew was ahead. And she badly needed that.

My mom was already grieving him before he was even gone. Every day, she watched the man she loved slip further away.

His voice faded to a whisper and never came back. He talked to people who weren't there. Thought he was at work, stocking shelves with cookies and crackers. He'd look at you and ask who you were—then remember again. And no one could tell her when, or if, he'd come back.

But one of the first doctors he saw after moving in with me didn't need a bunch of tests to see what was going on. I saw it in his face. The way he watched my dad. The way he avoided eye contact with me. He already knew.

We were sitting in the exam room when I decided I was done.

"Daniel, do you drink?"

He didn't answer right away. Just stared ahead like he hadn't heard the question. Like it didn't apply to him.

He stayed slouched in his wheelchair. Didn't flinch. Just his eyes—lifting slowly toward the doctor.

Then, finally, a whisper. "No."

Flat. Empty. Like lying came easy.

Dear Red Straw

My mom's eyes stayed locked on him. Her mouth was shut, but I could tell she wanted to say something—and couldn't.

That was the moment I finally just said it. I didn't care who was in the room.

"Yes. He drinks. A lot. He's been drinking his whole life."

"How much?"

"All day. Every day. He has to buy more every couple of days."

It didn't feel like power. It just felt necessary.

He couldn't hurt me anymore—not with his hands, not with his words. His mind and body were falling apart. And I was the one dealing with it now. The one taking him to appointments. The one cleaning up the messes. The one doing everything he couldn't.

No one talked on the way out. Not after everything I'd just said. Like I was invisible.

The drive home was quiet. He didn't bring it up again. Just walked in and poured himself another drink.

But the truth was coming—and a few days later, there'd be no denying it.

Jeremy Allen Damours

The morning we went back for the results, everything felt the same—same room, same chairs, same quiet dread. But this time, there was no guessing. We were about to hear the worst of it.

He clipped the films to the light and started talking. His brain was shrinking. There were empty spaces where parts of it should've been.

I knew what was coming next.

Then he said it—frontotemporal dementia.

It sounded as bad as it was.

It explained everything. The weakness. The confusion. The mood swings. The trouble swallowing. The slurred speech. The bad decisions. All of it.

My dad didn't react. He just sat there.

"Daniel, you have to stop drinking," he said.

"If you don't stop now, you're going to be wearing diapers for the rest of your life."

Then his tone softened.

"But if you quit now—today—you might be able to get back some of what's been lost. Not everything, but enough to function a little better. Enough to have some quality of life again. But you have to stop now."

My dad didn't say anything. Just gave a slow nod. But it wasn't a yes.

Dear Red Straw

"I'm fine," he whispered. Like he'd already given up.

My mom's eyes started to fill. Her lips gently quivered, like she was pleading with him in her head—wanting him to change, but unable to say it out loud.

He wouldn't let go of the one thing that was killing him.

In that moment, I think we all understood—this was it. There was nothing more we could do. He wasn't going to stop. Not for the doctor. Not for my mom. Not for us. Not even for himself.

And then we went home—and he made a drink.

I stood there and watched him do it like he always did. He tipped the plastic bottle over the edge of the cup and let it pour. Liquor sloshing back and forth. Topped it off with a splash of 7Up. He stirred the glass a little. Lined up the straw just right. Started sucking, then let it sit in his mouth for a second before swallowing.

Like a ritual. And that's what got me. Not the drink itself, but the way he still made it feel normal.

Like this was still his life to control. Like the diagnosis didn't matter. It was like watching someone light a match in a room full of gas— and pretend it's just a candle.

And things only seemed to get worse. The drinking picked up—more trips to the ice maker, more late-night refills, more runs to the liquor store.

Jeremy Allen Damours

It felt like he was speeding toward the end, like he didn't care how much damage he did on the way down.

He stopped trusting us. If my mom and I talked quietly in another room, he thought we were trying to put him in a nursing home—or making end-of-life decisions. He'd turn the TV down for hours so he could listen better. He'd yell from the bedroom, "I know you're talking about me!" or "I can hear you!"—even when we weren't.

If I left the house for too long, he thought I was setting something up—an intervention, maybe. If my mom took too long at the store, he thought she was cheating. He watched us for clues—our tone, our faces, our whispers—trying to piece together what he couldn't face. Like if he could hear it, he could stop it. But it only made things worse.

His body was getting weaker too. I told him to call for help before getting up, but he wouldn't. He wanted to show he was still strong, still able to do things on his own. He'd try to walk to the bathroom or reach for something across the room—only to fall. Over and over again.

It was becoming too much. We had hit a wall. We couldn't take care of him by ourselves anymore. We needed help.

So we brought in home hospice.

And with hospice came the one thing my dad wasn't ready to face—that he was dying.

Dear Red Straw

The chaplain's visits didn't help either. My dad wasn't religious. He didn't care for sermons, and he really didn't want to sit across from someone trying to talk him into believing it was really happening. To him, the chaplain didn't bring comfort—he was a sign that time was running out.

I didn't like the visits either. After everything I'd been through with the church—being pushed out for being gay—I didn't want anything like that in my home.

It wasn't the chaplain's fault, but still... it felt almost insulting. Like the same kind of people who once shut me out were now trying to offer comfort. Tidy prayers. Soft-spoken sympathy.

But this wasn't about me. It was about my dad. About my mom. About everything they were going through.

So when my dad stopped letting the chaplain see him, he started spending his visits with my mom instead. Praying with her. Talking about death like it was something peaceful. Something beautiful. Something to look forward to.

She seemed to get a little comfort from their time together. Maybe it was having someone to talk to. Maybe it gave her a small sense of order. Or just the feeling that someone was checking in on her too. Whatever it was, she looked forward to them. And I didn't get in the way—for her.

But even with those small moments of peace, things kept getting worse.

Jeremy Allen Damours

My mom was falling apart. But not so quietly anymore.

She was doing everything—feeding him, changing him, cleaning up after him. And the yelling. He'd scream at her for being too slow—bringing his drink, his antacid, helping him up, getting dinner on the table. And when dinner came, it was never right. Too late. Too cold. Overcooked. Not what he wanted.

At first, he'd calm down and tell her he loved her. But after a while, even that stopped. He didn't want hugs anymore. Didn't want her holding his hand or rubbing his back. He'd just look away. Turn on the TV. Say nothing. No apology. Just silence. And she'd sit there, like this was the new way she was supposed to love him.

One afternoon, she came back from the store carrying bags, her face wet with sweat from the heat. She looked pale. Tired. Her hands were shaking a little—probably from nerves or stress—but she didn't say anything. Just came in, set the bags down, and sat at the table. So I sat with her.

My dad started yelling from the bedroom. We couldn't even make out what he was yelling about, and my mom didn't seem to care. She just sat there, still, staring ahead. Whatever it was, she was done with it.

A minute later, he came out. He could walk sometimes, and today he was trying—moving slow, a little off balance, still yelling. Probably about the ice bag she hadn't put away yet. Said it was going to melt if she didn't hurry and get it in the freezer.

She didn't answer. Didn't move.

Dear Red Straw

He leaned up against the fridge, still yelling. And then, it happened—his body slouched, then his legs gave out, and he fell hard onto his side.

"Ow!" he screamed, like he couldn't believe he'd actually hit the floor.

My mom didn't even move. Her face didn't change at all.

She looked at him on the floor and, still sitting at the table, said, "Look what happened. You fell when you should've listened and stayed put." Her voice wasn't angry. It was just done.

I came out of my fog and grabbed the belt we used to lift him, but he wasn't doing anything. He just lay there—dead weight, silent. Maybe embarrassed. I couldn't get him up by myself, so I called Michael and the kids in.

Together, we dragged him back to his room and got him into a chair. All of us quiet. All of us pretending it wasn't as heavy as it really was—to lift him, to watch him, to keep doing this. I was fed up. Fed up that he was still acting like he was in control, even now. Fed up that I had to pull my kids into it. And at the same time, I didn't feel much. Just… present.

My mom was still at the table. She hadn't moved. Just sitting there, like this was normal now. Like she was giving up.

And it all just kept going downhill.

The trips to the emergency room started happening more often. Sometimes he'd fall asleep and we couldn't wake him up, and we'd call an ambulance.

Jeremy Allen Damours

Other times, he'd fall and say he was in too much pain to move, so we'd send him in to get checked out. Most of the tests came back normal. They always did.

Then he stopped eating. Days would go by, and barely anything. We brought up the feeding tube—he'd just shake his head. Didn't want it. Didn't want to talk about it.

I knew what that meant.

As a nurse, I should've known what was really going on—that we were past the point of fixing anything. I should've seen that the hospital couldn't do much anymore. And I did see it. I was hoping too hard. Panicking too much. Caught somewhere between what I knew and what I couldn't admit. This wasn't just another patient. This was my dad.

I thought they'd keep helping him. I didn't expect them to tell me to stop.

The last time he went to the emergency room, he was confused. Lost in his own mind. Something just didn't feel right.

We followed the ambulance and got to his side not long after he arrived. I was nervous. I kept thinking something bad was about to happen. But no one else looked concerned. The nurses were busy with other patients. The doctors didn't stop by. There was no rush. Like they had already accepted something I hadn't.

Then a doctor I'd talked with before—the one who'd treated my dad a few times—pulled us into the hallway. He looked me in the eye and spoke plainly. Not

Dear Red Straw

cold, but firm. Like someone who didn't want to say what he was about to say, but knew he had to.

"He has dementia. He's dying. There's nothing more we can do. Take him home. Keep him comfortable. Don't bring him back here anymore."

It wasn't cruel. It was honest. And it was exactly what I needed to hear. Because that's when I finally understood.

This wasn't going to get better. There was no fixing it.

There was only letting go.

And somehow, in that surrender, I felt something I hadn't felt in a long time. Peace.

Jeremy Allen Damours

"Don't bring him back here anymore."

Those words wouldn't leave my head. I didn't know how to fight them.

Until they led me to the railing.

It was late evening, just as the sky was letting go of the day. The last bit of sunlight hung like a bruise on the horizon—deep purples, fading oranges, a streak of gold barely holding on.

I stood outside, gripping the railing at the top of the stairs that led to our door. The metal was cold in my hands, but I didn't care. It felt like an anchor—something safe in the middle of everything falling apart.

I leaned into it, chest first, then let my head drop, resting on the frame. Letting it hold me—because I couldn't hold myself up anymore.

I started weeping.

Everything I'd been keeping inside—every moment pretending I was okay, every bottled-up scream, all the heavy steps just to get through another day with him in that house—came pouring out of me all at once.

I wanted to disappear. To run. To sleep for a year.

I needed someone to tell me it wasn't all on me. That I didn't have to choose between saving him and saving the rest of us.

Dear Red Straw

But I did. And knowing what had to be done didn't make it any easier. He couldn't stay. But putting him in a nursing home felt like giving up on him. Like I was failing him in the moment he needed me most.

And then—I felt arms around me.

Not a word. Just warmth. Soft. Caring. I didn't look up. I couldn't.

When the sobs finally slowed—when my hands could let go of the rail, when I could feel myself again—I knew.

He had to go.

Not because I stopped loving him. Because keeping him meant breaking the rest of us.

I woke up early the next morning, around 6 a.m. Something had me feeling like I needed to check on him.

I still felt the night before, but I knew what I had to do.

I walked into his room and found him sitting on the small couch next to his bed. Mixed drink in hand. Skinny red straw in place.

He looked up at me—eyes glassy, gray, distant. But not just from the alcohol. There was something else. He looked scared. But also calm. Like he'd made peace with something I couldn't see.

"I think this is my last day," he said.

I blinked. "What do you mean?"

"I think this is my last day," he repeated. "They're telling me it's time to go soon."

It was only a few days earlier when I walked into his room and heard him talking to someone—someone who wasn't there. He was speaking softly, and at first, it didn't make much sense—until he started saying names. Names of family who had already passed.

I didn't stop him. I just listened, chilled by the certainty in his voice.

So when he said, "they're telling me," I believed him.

I didn't ask for more. I just sat with him, letting those words sink in. I kept them somewhere deep inside.

All day, all week, I thought about them.

And I quietly started preparing myself. Not just because of what he said—but because of what I could see.

His body was shutting down. He hadn't eaten in over forty-five days.

It felt like the end was near.

Dear Red Straw

The day my dad left our apartment on a stretcher is burned into my memory.

It had only been a couple of weeks since he'd said, "I think this is my last day." I spent that time doing everything I could to find a nursing home that would take his insurance.

None of the options were fancy. We weren't looking for luxury—just somewhere safe and okay. I'd worked in nursing homes before, so I already knew not to expect much.

What worried me most wasn't how the place looked. It was the usual stuff: the smells, not enough staff, and how rushed everyone always was—like they didn't have time to make sure people were fed, clean, or even noticed.

My mom and I had carefully brought up the idea of a nursing home, but he said no right away. He was firm—he wasn't going anywhere. I couldn't blame him.

But we were all at our limit. He had to go.

By then, I'd been working closely with his home hospice nurse, and they came up with an idea that might make the change easier. His insurance would cover a week away—a short, temporary stay at a place where he'd still get hospice care.

We could just tell him it was a short break. Just some time away so everyone could rest.

The idea was that once he was there, the move into full-time care wouldn't feel so sudden.

It felt a little dishonest, but it was the only way that didn't end in everything falling apart.

To our surprise, he said yes—maybe because we kept saying it was only for a few days, or maybe because part of him knew we were all close to losing it.

But when the people came with the stretcher, that's when it really sank in. He looked scared. He knew exactly what was happening.

In one last try to hold on to control, he said he wasn't ready. Swore up and down he wasn't going.

But even as the words left his mouth, he didn't fight. Maybe he knew it was happening either way. He let them lift him onto the stretcher while they spoke to him gently, trying to make him feel safe.

My mom kept telling him it was just for a little while. That he'd be home again soon.

We all knew that wasn't true.

As they wheeled him out of the apartment, I'll never forget the way he looked at her—like she'd turned on him—and mouthed the words, "I hate you."

By the time he was moved to the second place—the nursing home where he'd spend the rest of his life—he was already in another world.

His mind got worse so fast in the next couple of weeks, he didn't even know where he was anymore. In some ways, that made things easier. Maybe, to him,

Dear Red Straw

there wasn't much difference between the nursing home and home.

Still, it broke my heart.

I remember visiting him that first day. He looked so small, so scared—tucked under the covers with the sheets pulled up to his chin like a child hiding from a monster.

Sometimes he'd have a moment of clarity—just enough to say, "I don't like it here. I'm scared of this place."

Then the fog would roll back in, and he'd start talking like he was back at work—stocking shelves, trying to get to his next delivery.

On some visits, he asked me to take him home. On others, he didn't recognize my mom at all. After nearly forty years of marriage, he forgot who she was.

Eventually, she stopped coming. She couldn't handle it—the smells, the sounds, the vacant look in his eyes. The fact that the man she loved didn't see her anymore.

It broke her.

There's one visit I'll never forget.

There was a Black woman in the bed next to his, hooked up to a breathing machine—unresponsive after a serious stroke.

My dad, in his confusion, thought she was his wife. He became protective of her. Every time she coughed or the machine made a sound, he'd call out gently, "It's okay, babe. You're okay. Everything's gonna be okay. I love you."

It was heartbreaking and oddly sweet.

Dementia had erased not just his memories, but even his sense of race. Of identity.

He didn't seem to notice that she looked nothing like my mom. Or maybe he did—and it just didn't matter anymore.

In his mind, she was someone he loved. And in that moment, that was enough.

I didn't correct him. I just sat there, taking in the strange tenderness of it.

Our last visit with him was on a beautiful Sunday afternoon—sunny, warm, the kind of day that almost tricks you into thinking everything's okay, even when it's not.

Michael, the kids, my twin brother, and I all went to see him at the nursing home. He was up and walking around that day. Still confused, still not making much sense—but stronger than he'd looked in months.

The nurse said he'd started eating again.

For the first time in a long time, I felt a flicker of hope. Maybe this was the start of one of those times where people with dementia seem to hold on for a while—sometimes even look like they're improving.

Maybe he'd live for months—maybe even years—in this place. Not ideal. But at least alive.

Part of me wanted to believe that.

Dear Red Straw

The other part knew this wasn't living. He wouldn't have wanted it to be this way.

Still, I let myself hope. For him. And maybe for me, too.

What I didn't know then was that this was the last time he'd have any strength at all.

Still, nothing about that day felt final.

As we were leaving, he did something I've never forgotten.

He walked with us down the hallway and stopped at the nurses' station. Everyone else had already gone ahead, but he reached out and gently held me back.

He asked if he could come with me.

I told him I'd come back soon to get him. It was a lie, but I said it to keep him calm.

I walked toward the door, then turned back.

He was still standing at the nurses' station, watching me.

We made eye contact.

He waved.

I waved back.

That was the last time I saw him alive.

Jeremy Allen Damours

A week later, I got the call.

I was in the bathroom, rubbing sunscreen on my face, when my phone suddenly buzzed hard against the countertop. I glanced over, expecting some random number. But it was the hospice agency.

They never called me on Saturdays.

My heart started beating faster. I stopped for a second, hands still covered in sunscreen. I didn't even wipe them off—just grabbed a towel with one hand, snatched the phone with the other, and answered.

"Hello, yes, is this Mr. Jeremy Damours?"

"This is him."

"Mr. Jeremy, this is the hospice agency. I'm really sorry to tell you this, but your father passed away this afternoon."

I didn't move. My brain couldn't catch up to what the man had just said. The words hung in the air, but I couldn't take them in. For a few seconds, I wasn't even in my body—I was watching from somewhere else, like it was happening to someone who wasn't me. I stood there, phone to my ear, my mind still stuck on the words.

It couldn't be true. My dad had been alive just days earlier—sitting up, walking around, talking. How could he be gone? Just like that?

"Wait. Wait—are you sure you're talking about the right person?"

Dear Red Straw

"Is your father Daniel Damours?"

"Yes, but... this is just so unexpected. I saw him a week ago. He looked better. Are you sure?"

"Let me double-check for you, sir. Sometimes we have the wrong patient."

The wrong patient? How do you get the wrong person during a death call?

For a second, I really believed it. That it had to be someone else. But then doubt crept in—maybe they were only double-checking because they could hear the panic in my voice. Still, part of me clung to the thought that it wasn't him. That this wasn't happening to my family.

The hold felt like forever. I kept hoping he'd come back on the line and apologize—that it was a mistake. That my dad was still alive.

But when he came back, his voice was calm. Final.

"No mistake. Your father passed away about an hour ago. I'm very sorry for your loss. We can only keep him here for another three hours before we have to release his body to the funeral home, so please come as soon as you can."

On the drive over, my mind raced. I've seen a lot of dead bodies as a nurse—some swollen, some sunken, some pale. Cold. Changing color. I didn't know what to expect. Not from him. I wasn't worried about how I'd handle it. I was worried about Michael. About the boys. I didn't want this to be how they remembered him—something burned into their minds forever.

Jeremy Allen Damours

When the man at the nursing home pulled the curtain back, there he was.

And he looked... peaceful.

I stared at his chest, watching for any sign of movement. Then I checked his wrist. Then his neck. Nothing. He was gone.

And then I did something I never thought I would—I touched him. I ran my hand over his arms, across his bare chest. I started talking to him. Said things I never felt safe saying when he was alive.

Tears started falling onto his skin.

All the walls between us—walls we'd built over decades—were just gone. In death, they didn't matter anymore.

The man who had caused so much pain, who shook the ground of my childhood with his addiction, was still. His fight was over.

And maybe—finally—so was mine.

For the first time, I felt a kind of peace. It didn't feel good, but it was there—mixed in with the sadness. Not because I'd forgotten what he put us through. But because something in me had finally let go. I wasn't trying to figure it out. I wasn't trying to fix anything.

I was just... ready to put it down.

But that wasn't the only heartbreak.

Some people reached out, but not many. There were no calls about a service. Just a few quiet check-ins.

Dear Red Straw

It didn't surprise me. It didn't make me mad. But it still stung.

Because deep down, I knew why.

My dad didn't build those kinds of ties. He didn't keep family close. He didn't make time for friendships. The only things he really held close were alcohol and work.

I'll never forget hearing my mom plead over his body before they took him away to be cremated. She was crying—telling him over and over that she loved him, that she was going to change, that she'd make him proud.

But change didn't come easy.

His death didn't end her struggles. For a while, it made them worse.

She wasn't just grieving the loss of him. She was grieving the loss of herself too.

When I carried his ashes back to Alaska, it felt unreal—flying across the country with a box that used to be a man. A man I loved. A man who hurt us. A man I still didn't fully understand.

But I knew where he belonged. Not in a box. Not on a shelf in my closet.

I took him to the banks of the Chena River—his favorite place. The same river he used to wander to at dusk, drink in hand, always with that skinny red straw poking out of the cup. I could still see him standing there, staring into the water the way he did when he wanted to escape the world—or maybe connect with something deeper.

That's where I let him go.

Into the quiet waters of the place he loved most.

There was peace in that moment. Not because everything made sense. Not because the pain was gone. But because it was time.

He finally belonged to something bigger than his struggle.

And in some way, I think he found the freedom he could never quite reach in life.

Dear Red Straw

When death moves in, it doesn't just take one person—it rattles everything around it. And when it's a parent who dies, especially one whose life was marked by addiction, it can feel both expected and unreal. You grieve the person and the pain. You grieve the love and the damage. You wrestle with guilt—over what you couldn't fix, what you didn't say, what you had to let go of just to survive it.

For me, my dad's death didn't bring full closure. But it helped me see things for what they were. I could finally stop trying to save someone who didn't want saving. I could finally let go of what I'd been carrying since I was a kid—the pressure to protect, to fix, to understand.

And I could finally forgive.

Not because it was easy. But because holding onto the pain any longer meant carrying a man who was already gone.

His death moved in slowly, then all at once. It tore through our home, opened up old wounds, and left behind space for something new to grow: peace.

Not the kind that forgets. The kind that accepts.

The kind that lets you breathe again. The kind that lets you keep living.

Jeremy Allen Damours

Dear Dad,

It hurts me when I close my eyes at night, lying in the dark, listening to the stillness. That quiet peace the night brings, when the world is asleep, when there are no expectations, when men are resting from their labors. That's when I think of you. And I hurt because you hurt.

I think about all those days and nights you spent feeling your body slip away, ravaged by a disease you didn't mean to invite in, but one that came anyway. You didn't expect alcohol to do what it did to you, not like that. You weren't a stupid man. You knew the life you were living would catch up to you eventually. But you couldn't have known it would take your mind the way it did.

It hurts me to remember the look in your eyes, how you reached for hope in a hopeless situation. How you feared death but couldn't escape it once it got a hold of you. It hurts because I'm scared of death too. You

Dear Red Straw

went through something I know I'll have to face one day. And that terrifies me.

Dad, there's only one time I can clearly remember you being truly happy, and that was when I worked for you at Nabisco. You became a different man at work. You treated me like a father should treat his son. You treated me like one of your employees—fairly, without judgment, without any of the weight we carried at home.

You looked out for me, lifting the heavy boxes when you saw me struggle, letting me leave early when I had appointments, making sure I was okay. You spoke to me with kindness and respect. You even treated me to lunch often, and we always found something to laugh about, joke about, gossip about. Those years we worked together, I'll cherish them forever. Because during that time, I had the kind of father anyone would want.

I'll never understand why that version of you didn't follow us home. But it doesn't matter anymore. Nobody can take those

Jeremy Allen Damours

memories from me. Nobody can touch what we had in those moments.

Thank you, Dad, for that time. For showing me who you could be.

And now, when I lay my head down at night, I comfort myself knowing you're no longer afraid of death. Knowing you've crossed over, and maybe, just maybe, you're waiting on the other side.

CHAPTER 11

STANDING STRONG

Being the one who holds it together
comes with a price.

When you're always the one others lean on,
it's easy to forget—
your needs matter too.

That quiet kind of leading
often comes with silence—
silence about your limits,
about when you're running on empty.

We learned to keep the peace,
to smooth over cracks,
to care for everyone else—
even when it drained what was left inside us.

For a long time,
we thought we couldn't say no.
We thought it wasn't our place.

At first, boundaries feel impossible.
"No" sounds selfish.
Standing up feels scary.

But over time,
we begin to see:
those who love us

will respect our limits.
Those who don't—
won't.

Slowly,
we stop living to please,
stop saying yes out of fear.
We learn to draw the line—
not to push others away,
but to hold ourselves close.

Some lessons come late.
But they come.
And when they do,
the picture becomes clearer.

We see that saying "no" isn't rejection—
it's protection.
It's wisdom.
It's strength.

And once we hold that line,
we realize something bigger:
we're not just surviving—
we're shaping our own way forward.

We didn't get to choose our childhood.
But we do get to choose
what we make of what it left behind.

The same parts of us that kept us safe—
watching closely,
guarding our feelings,
standing on our own—
can grow,
can soften,
can become trust,

Dear Red Straw

good judgment,
and quiet strength.

We don't have to be stuck
in the stories we were given.
We can honor where we've been—
without letting it hold us back.

We've already proven we can survive.

Now,
it's time to thrive.

Made in the USA
Las Vegas, NV
14 December 2025